COUNTRY TOWN BOY

REX ELLIS

Published by Boolarong Press,
655 Toohey Road
Salisbury Qld 4107
Australia.
www.boolarongpress.com.au

First published 2011

A catalogue record for this book is available from the National Library of Australia

ISBN: 9781925522709

Printed and bound by Watson Ferguson & Company, Salisbury, Australia

Foreword

Rex Ellis was born to travel. We have here an individual who has covered the length and breadth of Australia in many modes of transport. Albeit, one wonders how he has survived, with many excursions bordering on the brink of madness even to attempt such undertakings. But with much grit and determination he has pulled through with flying colours. His experiences, often in the media, show what an extraordinary fellow he is.

I believe that it all began way back in about 1948 when as a six year old he convinced me that a 'journey' should be taken. Consequently, a packed lunch was strapped to our three-wheeler bikes, and we were on our way. We travelled a full 2 kilometres down the main street of McLaren Vale from the Ellis house to Hardys Winery and back. Rex's mother, Joyce, nearly had a coronary on learning of the trip after the event. Mind you, the main street of McLaren Vale in 1948 was not the busy thoroughfare it is today.

This was the first of many trips. Rex often organised walks, either along the Willunga railway line or to one of the local nearby scrubs, and it was probably there that his ornithological interests began.

Another regular experience I recall in primary school days was playing 'parcel' along the main road out of McLaren Vale. Parcel is a trick game played on motorists, where a handbag was laid on the centre of the road. On seeing this, the said motorist would screech to a halt, and alight from the vehicle to retrieve the handbag, only to see it disappear off to the side, with a little help from some fishing line attached. Or, alternatively, we would wait for the motorist to bend over to pick it up, then snatch it from under his nose – resulting in many an upset motorist. But on a few occasions we were applauded for the trick. We played this for many years, until a near accident one day had the local constabulary put an end to it.

It was after the Second World War and Rex's father, Max, had just returned from overseas service – and therefore had army gear on hand. Consequently, Rex conscripted many young local kids and formed the 'Army Gang'. In no time the whole town knew about Rex and his gang – complete with uniforms, caps, badges, water canteens, the whole lot including rank for all members. It was harmless fun, until a few other local lads decided to the contrary and many a battle was had.

There are many humorous stories and jokes concerning Rex, and over the years none have lost anything in the relating. It's great to see a bloke with his 'full of life' attitude. Rex is still doing it all, with the ability to communicate and relate his lifetime experiences through this and previous books he has written.

Jim Ellis
Cousin

Chapter 1

Earliest Memories

One of my earliest memories involved getting up at three o'clock in the mornings, and accompanying my father on the milk round.

Dad and my Uncle Lloyd (Dad's brother) had a dairy farm at a little town south of Adelaide called McLaren Vale. They also had the milk round. I was around about four at the time.

Dad would catch our black stallion called Sambo, and harness him up to the two-wheeled milk float. All the milk was stored in cans up the front, and Dad stood on the tail board holding the reins. I would sit up on the deck among the milk cans. We would begin up the top end of McLaren Vale, an area that used to be called Glochester, and go from house to house. Dad would stop 'Sam', then taking a small can and ladle, would walk in to where the household billycan was, often on the gate or fence, or on the front verandah or porch. He would take the money out, put it in his money bag and then ladle the required amount of milk in. When he returned to the float, Sam would automatically walk on to the next house. Often he would leave a mound of manure (Sambo, not Dad!), a bit of added value for the householder's garden. Dad would call back to the dairy, which was in the middle of McLaren Vale in what is now Ellis Park, and re-supply with milk.

My next real memories began at my first day of school. It wasn't a good beginning and probably typified my attitude throughout my school days.

I actually hung on to the rear bumper of our Ford car as Dad went to drive off. Mum had to get out and 'unlatch me', giving me into the care of a teacher, all the time me bawling at the top of my voice. After the first few days I seemed to settle in okay.

Early in my life I had a big problem with banking, and this has sort of continued in many respects. I don't know why this was viewed as such a huge problem. Every Thursday was 'bank day', and we would have to take a two shilling piece, plus our bank book to school. I put on a hell of a tantrum at home when Mum was organizing me to do it. I distinctly remember one morning setting off up the dirt footpath of Field Street. Dianne, my young sister, would accompany me up to what we called the 'Fat Pole', a wooden telegraph pole, about thirty metres up the road from our front gate, before returning home. Even then I must have been a bit devious, because I devised a desperate plan to prevent myself from going to school on a dreaded 'Banking Thursday'. When I reached the Fat Pole, I threw myself against it, striking it with my head. I did this several times until the pain was sufficient to make me cry, then I ran back to the house, telling Mum I had a bad stomach ache. Such was my performance that Mum allowed me to stay home for the day. Eventually I got over this banking phobia.

McLaren Vale was located twenty five miles (forty kilometres) south of Adelaide. It nestled between the Willunga scarp of the Mt Lofty Ranges and the Gulf of Saint Vincent, in undulating hilly country. Often referred to as the rich valley, its fertile soils produced a varied agriculture, including vines, almonds, stone fruits, vegetables, grain

crops and grazing. There were areas of bushland scattered throughout.

The Onkaparinga River was the districts' northern boundary, with Pedlars Creek running through the middle of the area.

Surrounding towns were Willunga, four miles to the south, Aldinga, five miles to the south west, Noarlunga, five miles to the north, and McLaren Flat, three miles to the east. Adelaide seemed like light years away.

Aboriginals

When the Vintage came around each year, aboriginals from the Narangeri tribe would arrive from Point McLeay on Lake Alexandrina, to pick grapes. While their parents worked in the vineyards, some of the kids would attend the McLaren

Vale Primary School. This always added a new dimension to the lives of us regular students, livening up school life considerably.

There was one tall, well-built bloke called Harry Long, who went by the name of 'Persil'. The reason he scored that name was due to a particularly colourful incident. He must have taken exception to the colour of his skin, because he purchased several boxes of Persil washing powder. Putting them in a bath, he filled the bath with water, and hopped in, staying in there for as long as was comfortable. He finally emerged from the bath, hoping to be a 'white bloke', but was very disappointed with the result when he rinsed himself off.

I think us white kids would have been disappointed if 'Persil' had changed colour, because we looked up to him as a sort of hero. Like a few of his aboriginal mates, he excelled at football and cricket, but not at 'book learning'. What impressed us most, though, was that the Headmaster, a Mr Daenke, excused him from classes – except for drawing and other subjects where he showed some interest. At one time a contractor was bituminising the basketball court, and looking through the classroom windows, we could see Persil driving up and down the freshly bituminised court on a steam roller. We were green with envy, but full of admiration for Persil for having got himself in to such a position. I was hopeless at maths, but I was never excused from attending classes.

On one occasion Mr Daenke (who had a fine turn of phrase) told me I "had the brains of the average merino", and on another occasion that I was "pure ivory north of the chin!" In my twenties I had a lot to do with merinos when I was jackerooing on sheep stations, and only then realised the full import of that particular insult. He told a mate of mine, Ray Beaumont, that he was "as slippery and slimy as a sewer rat", which was a bit rugged I reckoned. That was only a few of the 'compliments' handed out.

At a 'Parents and Friends' meeting, one of the mothers, with her son's recent test paper in her hand, approached the Headmaster. Pointing to a large red ink N.H. scrawled across the test paper, she inquired as to its meaning. "No Hoper, lady, No Hoper", muttered Mr Daenke, as he stalked off. Wouldn't get away with it these days.

Getting the cane and other forms of corporal punishment were commonplace. A quite well respected teacher called Mr Chandler, had a somewhat unusual way of 'dispensing justice'. When he got annoyed with a kid, mainly boys, he would walk down the aisle and grab you by the chin. He would then shake your chin vigorously back and forward, causing your teeth to be in grave danger of being jolted out of their sockets. Never heard of such a thing before, or since.

On one memorable occasion, a mate of mine called Trevor Nottage was in the firing line. One of Mr Chandler's pet dislikes was kids standing on their desks to look out the high windows of the ex army transportable classroom. In this instance Mr Chandler had left the room on some errand or other, and Trevor had stood on his desk to see if he was on his way back. Well, he was, and spotted Trevor Nottage peering out the window. Trevor scrambled down in a hurry, sitting back in his seat, but knowing full well that he would be 'in for it'.

In desperation he decided on a bold plan. He slobbered all over his chin before the teacher entered the room, and just sat there staring straight ahead, the whole class keenly anticipating the coming punishment (as kids do). Mr Chandler walked straight in, and headed down the aisle to the hapless Nottage.

He attempted to grab him by the chin, but his fingers kept slipping on the 'slobber'. In annoyance, the teacher raised his closed fist, and bought the soft bottom of it down on Nottage's head, several times, almost hammering him into the floor like a nail. In retrospect, I reckon Trevor would have preferred to have his teeth rattled.

In summing up all this corporal punishment, it certainly did keep us fairly well 'in line' - I mean you knew how far you could push things before you got whacked, and I think in general at this school the teachers were pretty fair. Mind you, it had absolutely no effect on the boys from Point McLeay. They would get the cane a fair bit, often for not coming up to scratch academically, but it was 'water off a duck's back' for them. They didn't seem to feel it like we did, and this used to frustrate the hell out of the teachers, while we used to admire the aboriginal kids for handling it so well. One of the black kids had what we reckoned was a real good trick, that used to infuriate one of the lady teachers.

Aboriginal kids had a bit of a habit of letting the old 'bogeys' hang out of each nostril, in the manner of stalactites. Was never a problem before us 'whiteys' came along with our set of social etiquettes. Anyway, this little bloke (Staffy) had the neat trick of being able to give a violent 'sniff', and these bogeys would shoot back up his nose.

Then, to add insult to injury, he would sniff 'outwards' and they would shoot down under his nose again. Dunno how he did it, but he could have made a good career for himself in one of those freak shows that travel the country. The lady teacher would be beside herself and make Staffy extend his open hand to be belaboured by her ruler. Quite often when she finished he would shoot the pair of bogeys in or out, whichever the case happened to be. The only way she could have stopped him would have been to cut his head off. In the end, she would march him off to Mr Daenke for a caning, but that never seemed to upset Staffy.

He used to try and give us lessons in this dubious art, but none of us came close to it. In deference to the more squeamish reader, I won't record here some of the more disastrous effects of these attempts.

When the aboriginal kids went back to Point McLeay after vintage, we really missed them, but I can't say the same for the teachers.

I viewed going to church and Sunday school very much in the same light as going to school. Dad and Mum were religious to the extent that they went to church (Methodist) most Sundays. Dad sometimes played the organ when the main lady was sick or absent, but he was also partial to a few beers at the pub on occasions. Anyhow, I sort of grew up going to Sunday school, but I have to say I resented all that valuable time on the weekend being denied to other more interesting activities.

I had a few mates who were also expected to attend every Sunday morning, among them the three Oakley brothers, Alan, Greg and Kingsley. They also lived in Field Street, up the top by the main road, where their parents owned one of the General Stores. Alan was the same age as me, and was one of my good mates growing up, and also to a lesser extent Greg and Kingsley. The Store had a long backyard that stretched for a hundred or so metres down Field Street, complete with an old shed covered in Ivy, where we had a 'fort' on and off.

Anyway, getting back to the church thing, our lack of attendance there seemed to coincide with the time that half a dozen of us older boys were sitting up the back of a church service. (Which we were often obliged to attend.) We had a whole 'pew' to ourselves, and were seeing how far back we could lean on the long wooden seat, when we passed the centre of gravity and it, and us, came crashing backwards on to the next pew. This created a sort of domino effect and the last half dozen pews all went down in succession.

Caused a hell of a stir, and us blokes were the unwelcome centre of a lot of outraged attention. Mr Timberlake, the Minister, who wasn't a bad sort of bloke, walked down and suggested politely that it might be best if us lads waited outside for the rest of the service, and we were happy to oblige.

As far as I can remember, that signified the end of my church going days, and it was a great relief. I have to say, even though Mum and Dad would have liked me (and Dianne) to keep going to Church, they never pushed us into it. That was very much appreciated. Anyway, I'm getting a bit ahead of the story.

Dad had been in New Guinea during the war, and had bought back several long metal trunks full of 'souvenirs'. The contents were greatly varied, and an absolute treasure trove to a kid like me. There were boxes of both .303 and .45 calibre bullets, disarmed German and Italian hand grenades, a bayonet, dozens of copies of an armed services magazines called 'I was there', and other instructions manuals on various items. There were ash trays made from empty shells, and one large unarmed seventy five millimetre shell. Numerous Army clothing, including several of Dad's peaked hats, (he was a Lieutenant) a tin hat, plus uniforms. There was a pair of field glasses, an officers 'swag' and something I used for years in the Safari business – a large fabric covered metal officers enamel crockery box, full of enamel plates, and cups, etc.

My pride and joy for many years was a magnificent set of preserved New Guinea butterflies. Mounted on cotton wool with a light plastic seal. All colours, the largest being about a foot wide.

Anyway, I became interested in starting up an 'Army Gang' as about that time there were several groups of kids 'ganging up' and sort of going in different directions. I probably had an advantage having Dad's officer cap, and bolstered by Dad's trunk, I promoted myself to Captain (my enemies in the Rival gang called me 'Colonel Nut') and appointed Robert Hannan, a good mate, as my 'Sergeant'. He was more than capable of keeping the 'rank and file' in order.

'Snow' and 'Brinny' Smith, who lived down the McLaren Flat road, ran the rival gang, sometimes called the 'Air Force Gang', although they were a bit short of aircraft! They were a couple of tough kids, who we took pretty seriously. Not sure how it started, but we suddenly seemed to have these two opposing gangs, and this went on for a number of years. We would have been aged from eleven to thirteen at the time, and this 'war' lasted for two to three years, on and off. During school hours, hostilities had to cease, but after school it was 'war as usual'. We took it pretty seriously.

Our house was on the edge of town, alongside the railway tracks, with one of our paddocks acting as a narrow buffer between the tracks and our house. There was Station Road running between the railway track and our boundary fence, and between the fence and the road, a line of Sugar Gums and Radiata Pine trees. In the end pine tree, a few of us, including the Bosworth brothers (John and Peter), Trevor Nottage, Alan Oakley, Jim Ellis (my cousin) and Robert Hannan, built a 'fort' up near the top of the tree, about fifty feet from the ground. It consisted of a timber platform, with a sort of wall on two sides, constructed of timber palings from an old fence. We had a wooden box up there, which we filled with green pine cones. This was supposed to be our 'lookout'.

Below our house, we dug about four 'fox holes' around a metre deep, several metres long, and laid logs out along the side facing the railway. At one stage we had a giant shanghai mounted in front of one (our 'artillery'), consisting of a large timber fork, with pushbike tubes and a patch of canvas at the back to hold the projectile (a rock). Perhaps it's just as well this armament was never successful.

Behind the 'trenches' we built a hut constructed of old timber, and more palings we pinched off a fence down the McLaren Flat road one night. It was from a house near Smiths' place, and rated as another 'incident' to keep the war going. This hut was used for many things over the years, but during the height of the war, we called it a First Aid post. My sister Dianne was our Army nurse, and would often hide herself in there during the 'battle'. She had a good supply of band-aids to treat the 'wounded', but casualties were usually pretty light. There were three casualties that come to mind.

One of my 'troops' called Roger Dyer was hit under the bottom lip with a Daisy airgun slug, but he took off before Dianne could attend to him (she later became a theatre nurse at the Queen Elizabeth Hospital, so this training wasn't wasted!) Another bloke on the other side, called Barry Standfield, was hit under the eye with a slug, so he was lucky not to lose an eye. The classic though, happened on a hot Saturday afternoon. Snow Smith's gang was laying seige at our main trench area between our house and the Railway Station. It was a day of drama. Early in the afternoon, Trevor Nottage had been up the pine tree, manning our viewing platform. His job was to warn us when he sighted Snow's gang approaching. Their normal approach was along the railway, but on this occasion they came down Field Street, and caught Trevor unguarded. Before he could climb down the tree, Snow had run up and blocked off his escape route. We watched the little drama unfold as Snow slowly climbed the tree, all the time threatening Trevor, who was anxiously peering down from the platform. What happened next surprised everyone, especially Snow.

When Snow was only a couple of metres from the platform, Trevor grabbed a cardboard carton full of green pine cones that we kept up there, and upended the lot on top of Snow. Snow hugged the tree with pine cones bouncing off his head and shoulders, and flying past him. Behind the last of the pine cones came Trevor, passing Snow before he was aware of it, in his semi confused (and probably stunned) state. He reached the bottom in quick time and scurried up to the safety of the trenches.

Then the battle began in earnest. This was November and because it was around Guy Fawkes time, our armament was greatly expanded. We had 'hand grenades' that consisted of several Fourpenny 'cannons' strapped together with their wicks joined. They were effective, and good for sound effects. Our main 'Guy Fawkes' weapon though, was the 'Rocket Guns'. These consisted of a wooden stock with a conduit barrel, we simply stuck two and three penny sky rockets in the end, lit the wick and pointed it at the enemy. The results were varied but always dramatic.

It was late afternoon and Brinny Smith had made a bold charge up to our trenches and thrown a 'hand grenade' into our hut, which was the Red Cross Station. Dianne gave a squawk and Brinny ran back toward his line. As he did so, Alan Oakley aimed a rocket at him. It took off with a' swish', but did a big curve around to the left, hitting Billy Banks, who had his back to us, between the legs. It actually lodged there and exploded. A whole lot of smoke erupted from between his legs, and we saw him bolt behind a tree out of sight. Didn't think much more about it at the time.

The 'battle' sort of petered out around an hour before the sun went down with no real winners declared. Snow's mob did have a bit of a win though, in that they captured one of our' artillery pieces'. However with two blokes manning the thing, it was only possible to project the rock about 20 feet, hardly an effective deterrent. Still, they looked good, and we were all pretty shitty that we had lost one.

That evening I was sitting at the table with Dad and Dianne, and Mum was standing at the sink preparing the evening meal. It was just about dark. Mum said "who on earth is that?" and I went to the window for a look. Who it was, was Billy Banks. He was running from one tree to the next, and his pants seemed to be flapping around his bum. He soon ran out of sight. His problem was that when the sky rocket had exploded between his legs, it had burned his pants, underpants, and actually scorched his 'crown jewels'. There was a hell of a stink over this. His parents took him to the doctor the next day, and made quite a fuss over it. Vin Banks was the local barber, and rang Dad and complained about his son's injuries. I'm not sure how Dad responded, but I know Vin Banks told all his customers that it was a disgrace how these' gang wars' were allowed to happen. The Headmaster at school (a Mr Braur at the time) made a speech at assembly waffling on about the dangers surrounding these sort of activities. You would reckon if he was any sort of a teacher he would point out the character building benefits of such activities. Also the fact that we were saving the Government valuable funds in combat training!

Anyway, it soon blew over and everything got back to normal. I reckon my Army gang had a lot more discipline about it than Snow's gang. Admittedly some of them were a lot tougher boys, with the likes of Tony Rayner and Neville Perry amongst their ranks. But we were better organised, and actually had an 'infrastructure', something that you could attack. That is our hut and trenches.

***

Chapter 2

Early Criminal Tendencies

It's easy to see how some kids can go on and get involved in a life of crime. As a kid I can recall several incidents that could have been the catalyst.

One was Bill Price's watermelons. Bill and his wife were a childless couple that lived down the bottom of Field Street on the edge of town. He had a few acres of the Pedlar Creek Flats, ran a couple of cows and had a bit of a market garden. None of us lads liked him, because he didn't seem to like us – very unfriendly. But he used to grow great watermelons, and a few of us used to sneak down at night and steal some. We would generally sit amongst them and eat one, then carry away as many as possible (which wasn't many). He soon became aware of our activities, and on a couple of occasions caught us at it, and chased us. He couldn't run very fast so we became bolder and more regular.

One night he snuck up on us, and we saw he was carrying a gun. We dropped our melons and bolted. Suddenly there was a shot, and I heard Robert Hannan give a yelp. We went into overdrive and didn't stop running until we reached the back of our place. Robert had a sore bum where a couple of pellets had hit him. Bill Price had been using saltpetre in

his shotgun, and it certainly worked, because we gave that particular enterprise away.

Later on I had a nice little racket going pinching comics. Up the top of Field Street on the main road, there were two general stores – the Four Square Store and Oakleys Store. The three Oakley boys, Alan, Greg and Kingsley were all mates. In later life Kingsley became a Police Superintendent, but he missed a golden opportunity where I was concerned, in detecting me and instituting a 'citizen's arrest'. Anyway, myself and a few others would go into the shop and browse through the comics. This particular scam involved buying one comic. When we were ready to purchase the comic, we would place another comic inside the first, and march up to the counter, always choosing the more seemingly gullible assistant. It worked well for a long time, but eventually one bloke got too greedy, trying to put several unpaid for comics in between the paid one. The scam was 'blown' and we had to give it away.

My other successful criminal pursuit was going around to the back of the large Four Square store, selecting used soft drink bottles from where they were stacked in boxes. I would then take them around to the front of the store, and resell them. One day a Mr Brown caught me at it. Taking me literally by the ear, he led me down the footpath to our place, where he knocked on the door. Dad was home, and Mr Brown explained my actions and left me to Dad's 'mercy'. Dad was pretty wild, and I got a few belts with his razor strap around the legs, and sent to my room. So ended that devious operation.

The Railway Station

During my early years, the Railway Station was a big factor in my life, particularly as we lived on the edge of town, next to the Railway Station yards. A Mr Schroeder was the Stationmaster, and I had a pretty good relationship with him. There were two trains a day during the week that ran from the Rail head at Willunga, via McLaren Vale, Noarlunga, Morphett Vale, Reynella and into Adelaide. One was in the morning around seven a.m., and the other back to Willunga about seven p.m. But my favourite was the Saturday morning goods train, and the engine crew (driver and fireman) were my particular heroes. It was my ambition to become an engine driver when I 'grew up'.

Most Saturday mornings, after breakfast, I would go through our paddock and into the station yards, where the train would usually spend about an hour shunting. I would approach the cab of the steam engine, and yell out "can I come up?" All the drivers knew me, and up the ladder I would climb, into the magical world of the engine drivers. They would let me shovel coal, blow the whistle, and on occasions, even operate the lever to move the engine. I was in my seventh heaven, and couldn't wait to get old enough so that I could become a Loco driver. As it turned out I became a camel driver instead, but never mind that.

Trevor Nottage and I used to play a dangerous game with the evening passenger train. Making sure Mr Schroeder was in his office, we would jump on and off the last carriage as it gained speed alongside the platform. On one occasion Trevor left it too late to get off as it passed the end of the platform, and had to travel on to Willunga. He eventually plucked up courage to go into someone's house and tell them the story. They duly rang his parents. His father had to drive to Willunga and pick him up. He copped a hiding for that.

At certain times they used manual trikes or quads along the rail. These consisted of small platforms mounted on four wheels and were propelled along the line by pulling a large lever up and down.

One Saturday afternoon a few of us went for a joyride on one of these. We took it half way to Noarlunga where we left it on the line and walked home. This caused a hell of a stir, and we never owned up to it. We heard it had nearly caused a derailment, so we didn't indulge in that practice any more.

On another occasion a couple of us hopped under a culvert area, with the wooden sleepers and line less than a metre above our heads, and waited for the evening train. We heard it coming ages before it arrived, and then suddenly it was upon us. There was a huge noise accompanied by a cloud of steam as the locomotive passed above us, then the lesser racket as the carriages went across - just another 'railway experience' for us.

We would also commit the minor crime of putting pennies, and once a two shilling piece, on the line and letting the train flatten them. We heard later that it was a crime to deface the King or Queen's image, but those flattened coins were valuable bargaining items for us.

My crowning highlight in my early railway career, was when a couple of the crew let me ride in the loco down about a mile to where the line crossed the main road near the Hotel. I walked home feeling enormously proud.

Pedlars Creek

Pedlars Creek ran out of the hills up from McLaren Flat, along the north side of McLaren Vale and into the sea at Moana Beach. It ran every winter, sometimes flooding some of our land to the north of the town, and always had good waterholes in the summer. There was one small, but deep, hole that was the designated local swimming hole, and us lads spent a lot of time there in the summer. We would catch yabbies as well as small Blackfish and Congoli.

There was a bank about three metres high on the north side of the creek, and this is where we learnt to dive. Paul Chenoweth was probably the best of us perfecting an excellent jack-knife dive. A hundred metres down stream, Field Street crossed the creek on a bridge and this was the venue for many and varied meetings.

Ellis Brothers' (Dad and Uncle Lloyd, who was the local butcher) land ran along the creek to the north, and included an almond orchard on the steep hill overlooking the town, with the rest given over to share cropping and dairy cows. When Dad and Uncle Lloyd sold the dairy and milk round, they ran fat lambs there. The creek very nearly claimed a life a few years later when I was going to Boarding School in Adelaide. My young cousin, Craig Philbey (aged around ten) had been in the swimming hole with a few others on a hot Saturday afternoon. One of the kids ran into our place breathless and told Dad that Craig had gone under and not come up. It had taken him at least five minutes to run up to our house from the creek. Dad jumped in the car, tore down to the bridge, and jumping into the creek he began wading upstream. He trod on Craig and pulled him to the surface where he gave him some mouth to mouth. This was close to ten minutes after he had gone under, and amazingly he revived, and was none the worse for the experience.

The Onkaparinga River ran parallel to Pedlars Creek four miles to the north of us, and I would spend a lot of time up there in a year or two's time. My cousin Jim and I would sometimes go on what we called 'journeys', and some of these would take us down Pedlars Creek. We would take our lunch with us, and one day we walked right down to the sea where Dad picked us up.

Daryl Seaman and Kevin Houston were with us, other times we would walk over to a mate's place at Blackers Swamp, called Rod Branson. I had the 'hots' for his sister, Shayleen, who was a bit older than me and didn't know I existed. Bitter sweet moments.

At school a few of us sort of imagined that we had 'girlfriends' and the three most popular sheilas in our class were Gae Seaman, Raelene McBride and Margy Marston. I think I can speak for all the blokes in that we took more notice of these girls, and others, than we let on. There was something about them that we couldn't quite put our finger on (speaking metaphorically!) The girls, even at that young age, were well aware of the power they had over us, and used it in various ways.

Every year a circus would come to town, and we always rented out a paddock that ran back to the main road. Strangely enough, my first experience with camels occurred one afternoon down near our house. The circus had just arrived hours earlier, and animals were being pegged out. Two camels walked the few hundred metres down to a row of old almond trees that ran alongside Field Street. Dianne and I went out and sat on a big old field gate at the bottom of the row of almond trees, and watched them get stuck into the almond leaves. They gradually browsed down towards us and before I knew it one of the camels was chomping away next to my head. I was alarmed and fell off the gate, grazing my arm. The camel took no notice, and I certainly didn't realise the possible significance of the moment. But that wasn't the only event that this particular circus was to be memorable for.

Later that afternoon, there were a number of us lads up at the circus watching them erect the big top. The foreman came over and offered us five shillings each if we would help erect the tiered timber seating. We jumped at the chance and spent a couple of hours working on the raised seating, the top row being over four metres from the ground. We felt pretty important, and went home to tell our families over the evening meal. After tea we got dressed up, and went up to see the show, which began at eight o'clock. The circus was halfway through, and we were watching a trapeze act, everyone looking up in the air. I was sitting with Jim Ellis on my right side and Trevor Nottage on my left. In between 'Not' and I was a join in the seating. I turned to Trevor to make some comment on the act, and was amazed to see him slowly moving away from me. Not only him but all the people that were sitting on that section of seating. There was a hell of a crash, with yelling and screaming, as the whole section collapsed. There was absolute pandemonium.

When the dust settled, one lad had a broken leg, and there were a number of cuts and abrasions. There were several doctors present, and a couple of people were taken up to the hospital. The rest of the show went on when it was all sorted out. The circus apparently blamed us lads for not doing the work properly, but the real blame had to be down to the circus for not checking our work. Anyway, it was no big deal and a great talking point for weeks. No pathetic litigation like there would be today. They did offer to pay costs for the lad with the broken leg, we heard.

Another time there was a circus set up at the 'Ree' (sports oval) and a couple of elephants got away and went into

Mannings scrub, on the hill behind the oval. Must have scared the shit out of the local fauna. They were soon recaptured, but for years after we used to look at the deep tracks set hard where they had walked through some wet ground.

The Greasy Spoon

A lady called Mrs Nott used to have a little cafe in the main street opposite the Hall. She called it 'Notts Cafe' but us lads called it the 'Greasy Spoon'. We used to go there for milkshakes and other lollies. I think we were a bit hard on Mrs Nott, because she sort of didn't seem to like or trust us, and you probably couldn't blame her.

For a couple of years we went through the 'Phantom craze'. The Phantom comics were well known and came out regularly, and we would read them avidly. Then there was the 'Phantom Club'. Some comics had a coupon in, that you could fill out and send off for a small fee. For this you received a certificate of membership, with a catalogue. The most popular items were the silver and gold Phantom rings, consisting of a skull and crossbones with red eyes that glowed in the dark. We greatly prized these. Then, there were the 'rubber stamp' rings, and these were what we terrorised Mrs Nott at the 'Greasy Spoon' with. She was apparently a superstitious lady, and we took advantage of this. We had the cheek to tell her that her milkshakes were too dear. This provoked a negative reaction from her. Then someone said that bad things might happen if she didn't drop the price of her milkshakes. We didn't do anything for a day or so, then, when we were sitting at a table having a milkshake we pressed a rubber phantom ring against the wall above the table when she wasn't looking. Soon after we left. When we returned a few days later the mark was scrubbed off. We reckoned she seemed jumpy. Anyway we ordered some more milkshakes, and when she was busy with another customer, we put a couple of skull and crossbones on the wall under the table. This really freaked her out because she closed the shop the next day. No one knew where she was or whether she was coming back. The following day she opened up again, but wouldn't serve a few of us.

The next day at school the headmaster, Mr Braur, addressed our class and warned us boys in general not to 'tease or trouble' Mrs Nott. That was the end of that episode, but the rings were greatly valued for a long time after.

Chapter 3

The Pictures

Most Wednesday and Saturday nights there were pictures held at the local Hall. The feature showing was advertised on a board at the Four Square Store and at the Hall. I went most Saturday nights, and sometimes on Wednesdays during the school holidays. There was a bloke in charge there called Mr Morphett, and there was a sort of on-going war between a lot of us lads and himself. He acted like he was a pretty important sort of bloke, and I'm sure he ran the show well. That included disciplining us lads as well, for the greater good of all.

On almost every pictures night there would be some sort of 'incident'. He insisted that we all sit down on the hard seats in the first few rows, where he could keep an eye on us from the projector room where he was screening the film. We had several regular 'tricks' that we would get up to. Probably the most popular was the 'Jaffa trick'. When there was a particularly tense part in the film, one of us would tip a packet of Jaffas (red hard round lollies with chocolate centres) on the wooden floor, causing them to bounce everywhere making a hell of a 'din'.

Mr Morphett would come storming down from the projector room, work out who he reckoned was the ringleader, grab him and lead him outside by the ear, where he had to stay until the interval or the end of the flick. Although they wouldn't admit it, we reckon a lot of the adults (especially the fathers) use to enjoy the entertainment, because Mr Morphett was such a 'try hard'.

At one stage there was a great leap forward in technology with the advent of condensed milk in tubes. We soon purchased a few of these and one night we simultaneously squeezed a lot of condensed milk in the hair of the girls, who used to sit in front of us. That caused a fair bit of flack from parents, and condensed milk tubes were banned from the hall after that. As were water pistols when we had a session with them.

In between all this goings on, we used to very much enjoy the picture shows.

***

Chapter 4

Playing Parcel

Playing 'Parcel' has been practiced by generations of kids, although as I write I reckon it's just about done its dash. It would be classified as a hazard to traffic under the Road Traffic Act no doubt.

We used to play this game at various times, and two particular incidents come to mind. The first occurred on the road between McLaren Vale and Aldinga near a low cutting the road ran through, not far from Sherriffs Farm. It was a fairly isolated spot and there was good cover in bushes by the side of the road. We would place this handbag on the road, with a length of catgut (fishing line) attached to it. Then we would sit among the bushes and wait for our first 'customer'.

On this occasion, we waited around twenty minutes before we saw a brown Chev sedan approaching at a fair old bat. It was almost onto the handbag before the driver spotted it and slammed on his brakes. It took the car a good hundred metres to pull up, but as soon as he was past, we pulled the bag in. Meantime, the car had pulled up and was backing up. When the driver got to where he reckoned the object was, he pulled up, and got out of the car. It was a young bloke in his twenties. Then the passenger door opened and what

was probably his girlfriend got out and joined him. We could hear them talking. The bloke was swearing black and blue that he had definitely seen a handbag on the road, and his girlfriend obviously didn't believe him. After a while they hopped back in the car and drove off. That was fairly typical of what used to happen and it was always good for a laugh.

That afternoon, we had caught three cars, and were just about ready to pack up and go home, when we heard another car approaching at speed. It was a red sedan going like the clappers. It began braking about fifty metres before the handbag, and skidded to a stop around forty metres past. We whipped the bag in and waited. A fairly tough looking bloke got out, and started walking back. He reached where the bag was, then stopped and looked directly at where Alan Oakley and I were hidden. He then started walking towards us. We held our nerve until he was about twenty metres away, and then got up and bolted. We knew he was chasing us, as we scrambled through the fence and headed into a paddock full of wheat almost ready to reap. I took a glance over my shoulder and saw that we weren't increasing the space between us. Fear is a great accelerant, and our turbo chargers kicked in.

After probably half a kilometre he was still following us, but we had greatly increased our lead. Soon after he stopped and we saw that he was heading back to his car. With great relief we pulled up and fell to the ground pretty well buggered. We weren't game to go back to our push bikes that were left near Sherrifs Farm, but instead walked home across the paddock to McLaren Vale, getting home before dark. I'm not sure what Alan told his parents, but I told Mum and Dad we both had flat tyres on the bikes and decided to walk home. They seemed to accept that okay.

On the second occasion, I was playing Parcel with my cousins, Jim and Richard Ellis. We had a great spot right in the middle of the town, in a thick pine hedge, at Jim and Richard's place. We had hollowed out a spot inside the hedge, and it was the perfect spot, very difficult to observe from the road because we would only access it from inside the dairy property.

It was a Saturday afternoon and we had already caught a few cars. We heard a motorbike coming, and saw a speed cop approaching. We hastily pulled the bag in, but it caught for a second or two in the hedge, before we managed to drag it in. The speed cop rode past without slowing his pace. We waited for about ten minutes, then went around and put it out again. We were only just back inside the hedge, when the cop suddenly rode back quickly, and pulled up by the bag that we had begun to pull back in. We sat inside the hedge, frozen stiff. The cop switched his bike off, reached inside his jacket and pulled out a packet of peanuts. He put some in his mouth and began chewing them. Then he casually said "You'd better come out here fellas, I want to have a yarn with you". We looked at each other, and slowly walked out, around through the gateway and up the road to where the cop was sitting on his bike, eating peanuts.

We walked up to him and stood there sheepishly while the speed cop finished his mouthful of peanuts. We were all pretty apprehensive.

He was wearing sunglasses and looked pretty cool. He finished his mouthful and holding out the packet of peanuts, said "Have some peanuts boys". We tentatively took some, and before we could put them in our mouths, he said "You know, I used to play Parcel when I was a kid - good game isn't it?" I think that we all nodded in the affirmative.

He continued, "Only trouble is, it could easily cause an accident, you know another car running into the back of the first one". We all nodded."Yeah, so you better not do it again fellas - you wouldn't want to cause an accident, would you?" "No", a couple of us said."Anyway, it's been good meeting you boys, and I'll be on my way now". He handed Jim the remainder of the peanuts. We watched in awe as he kick-started the big Triumph, clicked it into gear with his foot, and took off fast, heading down the road. Richard said "I think I might be a speed cop when I grow up".Anyway that was the last time we played Parcel in the town.

***

Chapter 5

Yorke Peninsula Holidays

Every year after Christmas for a number of years, Dad and Mum would hire a caravan, and along with Horace and Linda Poole, would head over to Stansbury on Yorke Peninsula. It was a quiet little town with fishing and farming the main industries, as well as catering for tourists. We would hire the caravans in Stansbury, and spend a couple of weeks in the caravan park along the foreshore. I remember a long hot drive with Dianne and I sitting in the back seat of the Holden, and often having arguments. Dad would sometimes reach over and land a whack, usually aimed at me.

On one occasion a very alarming thing occurred, and we were very fortunate to get away with it. We had only just left home, and were driving along a straight stretch of road between Noarlunga and Hackham. Dianne must have been playing with the door handle, because all of a sudden it flew open. I looked across and saw her hanging grimly to the door. Dad immediately pulled to a halt, but we would have travelled about a hundred metres with her hanging on the door. Just before the car pulled up, Dianne dropped to the road, luckily missing the rear wheel. She had a few cuts and abrasions, but wasn't seriously injured. After that, Dad made sure all the doors stayed locked when we were travelling.

We always looked forward to the stays at Port Wakefield, where we would have an icecream and a cold drink. Then as we drove south down Yorke Peninsula, Dad would always make the joke about there being no snow on the Hummocks. They are the highest point on Yorke Peninsula, all of a couple of hundred feet above sea level. Finally we would arrive at Stansbury, get the caravans organized and unpack the gear. Sometimes we would hire a shack from the Gill family, and I would camp in a tent out the back, sometimes with a mate.

On one occasion Alan Oakley came with me, and in the late afternoons we would go with Dad rabbit shooting. We got plenty of practice with the .22 rifle, and really used to look forward to these shooting trips. I was always a dead keen bird watcher, and was as far back as I could remember. At first I was only interested in parrots, and the thing I wanted most in the world was a South American Macaw. I just had a thing about them, and had a big colour picture of one in my room. Gradually though, I became interested in other birds as well. Stansbury was a good place to observe sea birds, from the various waders that used to congregate on the long sand spit at low tide, to the Crested Terns along the foreshore.

Near where we used to stay, the Gill family had a fish and chips shop, as fishing was their main occupation. I've had a bit to do with marketing my own business, but I never forgot the most simple and effective marketing I have ever seen. On the front of Gill's fish and chips shop was a big sign. It said "Fish Have Gills and Gills Have Fish". I reckon it was a winner.

Mr Alf Gill was an old fisherman that could often be seen standing stooped on the beach in his old hat and black coat looking out to sea. He would spend half an hour without seeming to move. We would go up and talk to him and he told us a lot about fish, and the best place to fish near to shore. We had the use of a wooden dinghy, and some nights we would go out with a tilly light on the bow, and spear Flounder in shallow water. They were delicious eating.

One year we drove down to Edithburgh on the 'foot' of the Peninsula, and Dad organised the Mail boat that took the weekly mail and stores to the lighthouse keeper on Troubridge Island, to take us with him. I really enjoyed that day, mainly for the hundreds of nesting pairs of Crested Terns and Silver Gulls. I took a lot of photographs, and thought that Troubridge Island would be an exciting place to live.

For a few years running, Wendy Poole (the eldest daughter of Horace and Linda Poole) bought a friend with her called Merleen Webber. Alan Oakley and I were both sort of besotted with her. She used to wear very brief bikinis, had long tanned legs and sort of reduced us to stuttering idiots. In a way we would like to be around her, and in another way it was a relief to be away somewhere else. Still a very mysterious area for us young blokes. Wendy was also an attractive girl, but friendly.

Large wheat ketches used to arrive regularly at the Stansbury jetty to load wheat and barley from the local farms, and these used to fascinate us. We would go and talk to the crew and watch the loading, and sometimes they would let us go aboard.

One year I had received a spear gun for Christmas, and I couldn't wait to try it out. A few days after we arrived at Stansbury, I was walking along the beach when I saw a large stingray travelling along parallel to the beach. I couldn't resist it, so I cocked the gun and fired at it from the beach. The spear lodged just above its tail. Almost immediately its tail flashed and cut the cord. The last thing I saw of the stingray was it heading out to sea with the spear sticking up in the air like a beacon. I wasn't able to get another one over

there, and had to spend the whole holiday without using the spear gun. Serves me right I suppose.

They were all good memories.

***

Chapter 6

Christmas Eve

Christmas Eve was always a big deal for us kids. Every year a show was held out the front of the Four Square Store. I think the Hainz family might have started it and when the Seaman family bought the business, they continued the tradition. The event consisted of a Christmas tree, with Father Christmas, but the big event was the reindeer and sleigh that bought Father Christmas to the show. It consisted of two blokes, one standing up straight, wearing the new head and antlers, and the other bending over, making up the back and hind legs. That was hard work in the rear end.

Well, one year the job was up for grabs and myself and Trevor Nottage scored it. It was pretty prestigious, and we were tickled pink. I told Trevor that he had better be the back and hind legs, as he was taller than me, and that a reindeer with a tall neck and head, with a short back would look ridiculous. He wasn't keen because the rear end had to travel blind, but my logic seemed to convince him.

We arrived up at the back of the Four Square Store an hour before Father Christmas was due, and had the suit fitted -that is we got into it. Felt pretty weird. We had a bit of a dummy run around the yard, and got the hang of it, although Trevor kept complaining that his back hurt, and he couldn't see anything.

Then 'Father Christmas' arrived, a bloke called Morry Robinson, who was a very regular and popular Father Christmas. Every town has blokes like this.

He hopped in his sleigh, and we headed off around the block. I was going okay but Trevor was having trouble with his back, and didn't like the fact he was travelling blind. Father Christmas kept giving him encouragement, like he was the 'backbone' of the operation, but it was falling on deaf ears.

When we arrived back at the Christmas tree there was a big noisy crowd gathered. Everyone seemed full of joy and fun, except the rear half of the reindeer. We moved through the crowd, and then I observed a bloke poke the body of the reindeer (Trevor). I heard Trevor curse. Then he did it again. This was too much for Trevor. He lashed out with his boot and got this bloke in the ankle.

He gave a howl and hopped away, but Trevor seemed to enjoy venting his frustration, and kicked out again getting someone else I couldn't see. This caused official action, and some bloke who I didn't know, came up and addressing the head of the reindeer (me) began lecturing us.

This caused an attack of the giggles from me, and with more whining from Trevor, the reindeer was led away to pasture. That was the end of our Christmas 'career'.

***

Chapter 7

Trapping Rabbits

I made my first money trapping rabbits. I used to set about a dozen traps on the north side of the Railway Station yard, and gradually moved further north on 'Spongs Hill' and into Mannings Scrub, behind the oval. I would set them after school, and get up around five am, going around them before school. I had my regular customers in the town, selling them for 3/6d (three shillings and sixpence) each, which was very good money for me.

I had a male whippet dog called Jock. He was a great mate and character. Most days when I was at school he would head off on his round to various charitable households who would give him a hand out. His most important stop was at Uncle Lloyd's butcher shop, where they used to really spoil him. One day when I was walking home from school, I came across him half way down Field Street, towing this huge bone as big as himself. He was determined to make it home with it, and he did.

Sometimes I would set wire snares under the run-throughs in netting fences, catching the odd hare as well as rabbits. Later on I took to carrying my Daisy air gun, and managed to shoot a few rabbits in the head if I could get close enough.

Later on, another money making enterprise presented itself – picking olives. Living in a Mediterranean region, meant that there were wild olive trees all through the McLaren Vale area, many of them growing along the minor roads and section lines.

A bloke called Dave Farley had a farm called 'Sea view', north of McLaren Vale above the Onkaparinga Gorge. He had an olive plantation on the property, and set up a crushing plant. As well as his own olives, he would buy them in, and he agreed to take any we could pick. Myself and different mates would go out on the weekends, with a large hessian sheet, a couple of old almond knocking sticks, and a couple of wheat bags. Once we got a bit of practice, we managed to pick a wheat bag in a day. We were paid two pounds a wheat bag, which we split in two, and I've never felt so rich since. It was pretty full on but we felt very proud of ourselves.

Later still, I improved on that. On some Saturday mornings I would ride my pushbike three miles out to McLaren Flat, and then another three to Blewitt Springs to a fruit block. The Adam's family gave me a job doing all sorts of jobs, from picking fruit, to pulling down old fences. They paid me thirty bob a day and I felt wealthier still. My faithful little whippet (Jock) ran along with me, and spent the day chasing rabbits.

One day I knocked off, and a mile down the road I stopped while Jock took off after a fox. I waited an hour and he didn't come back, so I left my coat on the ground and rode home. Dad drove me back there the next morning, and to my great relief there was Jock curled up like a ball, sound asleep. He was pretty pleased to see me.

On other occasions I would do a bit of work for a bloke called Frank Poole, who had currants.

We had about seven acres of old almond trees on a hill overlooking McLaren Vale on the north side of Pedlars Creek. Most years I would help knock these. There were no mechanical harvesters then, and we used to put large hessian sheets on the ground under the tree. We would then knock the trunk of the tree with a rubber knocker, consisting of a piece of inch pipe, a metre and a half long, with a hard rubber on the top end of it. After that, we used long sticks to knock the rest of the almonds off the tree. It was always done in the hottest part of summer, but I think I preferred it to picking grapes. I alleviated the boredom by watching birds when they were around.

One day I was doing some almond knocking with Duffy Sigston. He was not a 'birder' as such, and I was trying to encourage him by offering amounts of money if he could name a particular bird. I never took any risks with common birds. He hadn't named any, and I got cheekier and cheekier with the amounts offered. Suddenly a Black Shouldered Kite dropped on to a very large spider nearby. "Thirty dollars for the bird", I said. "Black Shouldered Kite", replied Duff, causing me to drop my knocking stick. Took me by surprise, but I had no option but to pay up. Gave that particular game away for a while.

This hill was pretty hard to work being quite steep. We used to have a lot of fun here with home-made 'sleds' made from sheets of corrugated iron, with the ends turned up. It was only a distance of about fifty metres, but we used to travel with great speed.

Quite a few summers in December, I would go up to Leo Oliver's White Hill Farm, picking apricots. Leo was a great character with a very robust sense of humour. There were often at least a dozen of us out in the orchard, a lot of us young lads, and older married women.

We were always mucking around, and quite often us lads would put about a dozen apricots in the air at once, aimed at the women's section of work. It never seemed to bother anyone including Leo, who would throw the odd apricot himself.

Amongst the women was a lady called Joyce Hill, very much a character in her own right – a quite excitable lady. This particular day we were sitting in the shade of the homestead's wide verandah, having lunch, when Joyce jumped up and headed for the toilet. Now, there were two outside toilets, but unbeknown to Joyce, one of them wasn't in use. It was the older one all covered in Ivy, but when you opened the door, it looked like it could have been operable.

We were sitting there eating our lunch when we heard some screaming, and Joyce came flying around the corner with her knickers around her ankles, in a hell of state. "I've been bitten by a snake", she yelled. "Where abouts?" said Leo. "On the bum", yelled Joyce, "Come and have a look", as Leo fled in horror. When it all settled down there was a simple non threatening explanation. The out of use dunny was occupied, under the seat, by a broody hen. When its' daylight was suddenly cut off it reacted as a broody hen would, giving Joyce two sharp pecks on the bum! It made our day.

***

Chapter 8

Nantawarra

I had an uncle and auntie who lived on a farm at Nantawarra, in the mid north, and sometimes would go up there for a week or so in school holidays.

I had this thing about getting a galah for a pet, and for some reason I can't explain now, thought that the best way to get one was to 'wing it' – that is, shoot it in the wing, get the wing fixed, and then make a pet out of it. Sheer madness, but that's what I was set on doing at the time.

My uncle would loan me a single shot .22 rifle for shooting rabbits, and this was what I intended winging the galah with. Well, I never got my galah by that means, because I was so conscious of doing it mortal damage that I always aimed too high. Probably just as well.

One time up at Nantawarra, there was a mouse plague. You need to experience one to know how frustrating they can be. Everything you lift up, mice pour out from under, and there is a general stink of mice. My uncle made a number of large traps where the mice could get in, but not out. I had a small stock whip at the time, and each morning I would take one of these traps out to the middle of the large open yard, and upend the trap. Dozens of mice would pour out and head for cover. I would get amongst them with the stock

whip, and disposed of as many as possible before they got to cover.

I spent many happy weeks at Nantawarra.

***

Chapter 9

The Beach

Because we only lived five miles from the beach, it was a big part of my growing up. Some of my earliest memories are of Dad going down to Sellicks Beach with Bill McMurtrie and others, pulling nets. Mum and Dianne would often go with us as well, and because these beaches allow cars on them, this is where I learnt to drive.

Mum would teach me, while Dad was out pulling the net, and it was a good place to learn, as nothing much could go wrong. Then, after the men had rowed out with the net and were heading in towards shore, we would all wade out into the water and help drag the net into the beach. There were always fish. It was good fun.

Another incident that might offend the more sensitive reader occurred at Moana Beach. There was a group of us, blokes and sheilas, in a little group talking in water up to our necks. As usual, us fellas were trying to impress the girls, which is why what occurred could only be described as 'challenging'. I noticed Trevor Nottage swim out to sea, and shortly after, swim back to the group. About ten minutes later this 'object' floated towards us. Several had to move in order to let it pass. Not a lot was said, but it was noticed that

Trevor had a very red face. You can't be too careful with these matters, because they can come back to haunt you.

Our closest beach was Moana, and very often on hot weekends or in the evenings through the week, we would all hop in the car, and drive down there. On this particular day, Dad was doing some body surfing, as he often did. He got 'dumped' by a big wave, and lost his false teeth. So he stood up with his legs together, bent down and placed an open hand on either side of his feet, and waited. The wave petered out near the beach, returning as undertow. Next thing Dad stood up, holding his teeth in the air. A hundred to one chance had rolled his teeth back to him!

We had one of those rubber blow-up 'surf shooters', and often used to see how many of us could fit on it, before being carried in by a big wave. Always good for a laugh.

Digging out bogged cars was another good pastime, and most days there would be one of these.

A few years later when we were in our teens, a few of us including Jim Ellis, Paul Chenowith, Robin Binney and John Sears drove down to Moana. Paul had his dad's V8 Ford Pilot car. It was at night and we noticed the local electrician's (Peter Anderson) car parked on the cliff top up the north end of the beach. He was a little plump short bloke, who was often referred to as 'Pinocchio' or 'the hat' (because when he drove past in his old Holden Station wagon, he was so short that you could only see his hat!)

At the time he was courting a girl, strangely enough called Marlene Anderson, who was in the car with him. It was a cold windy night. Not sure whose idea it was, but we all crept over to the back of the car, and together, picked it up. We then moved it toward the cliff edge.

Suddenly the driver door opened and 'Pinocchio' flew out wearing only a short singlet. He bolted, leaving Marlene to her fate. We dropped the car and also bolted. The word soon got around about this incident. Eventually the Andersons were married, but the word was that Marlene never forgave Peter for abandoning her. Lust or love just wasn't strong enough to stop Pinocchio from shooting through. Preservation is often a stronger emotion.

***

Chapter 11

Pets

From my earliest days, I had a number of varied pets. The first belonged to the family, a wire haired terrier called Terry. Eventually he had to be destroyed as he became a sheep killer which is not tolerated in the country.

Then, when I was around ten, I had a young nanny goat, called Nancy. Just a kid. She became my ever present companion, and used to follow me everywhere when allowed.

I remember one Sunday I went for a walk up into the scrub on Spongs Hill, which overlooks McLaren Vale. This is located near the recreation ground, and on this Sunday, a picnic party was there – city people transported by a couple of coaches. I was walking quietly through the scrub when I observed movement through the bush. Creeping forward slowly with Nancy at my heels I saw two people lying on a rug on the ground. What's more they were naked. The man was lying on top of the woman, and both were moving in an unusual way. I was mesmerized, having no idea what they were up to. I had some vague idea that it had something to do with 'making babies', that wasn't spoken about in public.

I think Nancy must have moved, or made a noise, because then suddenly the man sprung up with a yell, looking straight up. The girl sat up pulling the blanket around her.

The man roared something and began running towards us, a frightening sight.

I took off with Nancy at my heels. I ran for my life. I don't know how far the enraged nudist followed me, because I didn't waste time looking. I never told Mum or Dad about this incident, but discussed it at length with my mates, further fuelling our interest in this mysterious thing called sex.

Nancy tragically died of bloat.

Then, at the same time I had a young magpie called 'Fos' (named after Fos Williams, captain/coach of the Port

Adelaide football team that I barracked for) and a whippet pup called Jock. We bought him from George and Shirley Saurbier, who also used to drive Peugeot cars, something that I have continued to do all through my adult life. George and Shirley had a son called Jock, so I named my whippet after him.

Right from the start Jock was a great character. He wasn't the usual brindle colour, but brown and white.

Jock was my faithful companion for many years, accompanying me on most of my bush trips. Later I would go hunting rabbits, foxes and hares with him. I shot most of them with a 12 gauge shotgun (when I got my licence) but on occasion he would catch something himself, including once, a hare. Normally hares would get away from us, unless I was able to get it with the shotgun soon after we put it up. Often Jock would be in the way so I couldn't shoot. The whippet is the fastest dog there is, in the first thirty feet. They are flat our right from the start, whereas a greyhound has to 'wind up'.

Jock would follow the hare in a straight line, but if he ever got near the hare, the hare would suddenly head off at a tangent, making up a lot of ground. On one memorable occasion, when Jock was around five metres behind the hare, he suddenly shot out to the right. At the same time, so did the hare and Jock got it. He somehow must have sensed the hare's move. I was almost sorry for the hare, because I have a real soft spot for them.

On another occasion, Jock nearly lost his manhood. When chasing animals and coming to a fence, without seeming to break stride he would jump between the top and second wire of the fence. On this occasion they were both barbed, and when I caught up with him, I noticed blood on the ground under him. On inspection, I saw a deep red cut on the bottom of his scrotum, a very close shave.

Jock lived to a ripe old age – for a 'working dog'.

After Fos the magpie, I obtained a young crow that I called Jeckle. He was a good mate. My main memories of him are of me coming home from school. I always had a piece of meat in my pocket for him. He would be regularly sitting on the front gate post, waiting for me. He would fly on to my shoulder, and I would give him the meat. In appreciation he would, more often than not, shit down my back, but I didn't mind. Not sure how he died.

Next came a galah called Gus. He would fly free around the back yard, and often accompany me on my motorbike. One Saturday morning I was riding down the main street of McLaren Vale, when Gus suddenly took off and flew under the front of an approaching truck. I was devastated.

For a long time we had an Adelaide Rosella called Butch in a large cage by our back door, and in the same period Dad bought me a pair of Budgerigars. The male was a wild green one, called Crackers, and the female a bred blue one, called Priscilla.

I had them in a cage next to Butch, but after a while would let them out. They would fly around outside and always return to their cage to be locked up at night. They would often sit on Dad's shoulder of a late afternoon when Dad would be standing at the bottom the tank stand, reading the paper while he hand pumped water up to the header tank.

When the gums were flowering, all the Lorikeets would arrive in the area, feeding on the nectar, and would be around for several months. Then they would leave, and it was at this time that Crackers and Priscilla disappeared. I was very upset, but after a while I got over it. Then the next year, the Purple Crowned, Musk, and Rainbow Lorikeets returned again for the flowering.

A few days later we were sitting inside having tea, when I heard a budgerigar calling outside. I jumped up from my chair and went to the back door, and to my amazement and delight, saw Crackers sitting on the tank stand. I went out and he flew down on to my shoulder. All the family were thrilled. We fed him and put him in the cage for the night, noticing how he was a much brighter green. We kept letting him out in the day time, and I wrote to the famous naturalist, the late Crosbie Morrison, telling him about Crackers and Priscilla's 'adventure'. He wrote back saying that Crackers was probably a 'homing budgerigar', and that he knew of another example of this in the Duke of Bedford's collection in England. He thought my two had gone away with the lorikeets and returned (which didn't make a lot of sense because they feed on different things), and that a hawk or falcon probably took Priscilla because of her unusual colour (which did make sense). I kept this cutting in my 'What Bird is that?' bird book for years. Sadly a month or so later we had a violent storm. Cracker's cage flow over and he was killed. I was heartbroken.

More often than not, pet birds or animals that are allowed to roam free have a violent end. But it's probably better to have a short interesting life, than a long boring one in total captivity.

***

'Desert Head' caning McEwin

'Desert Head' caning John Manly (Basinhead)

'Desert Head' ordering some poor unfortunate wretch out the front to be caned

'Desert Head' caning Jim Bastion

'Desert Head' caning 'Tadpole'

Onkaparinga Gorge, North of McLaren Vale

Pedlars Creek

A 'Journey' (Cousin Jim Ellis on right)

Trapping Rabbits (Myself setting a rabbit trap)

Myself with Jock & Gus

Myself with 'Fos'

Dad & Dianne at Seal Bay on Kangaroo Island

Myself in Forresters 'Uniform'

Myself on 'Gypsy' in the Mustering camp on Elkedra

Myself 'studying'

Robin Binney, Paul Chenoweth, Jim Ellis and John Sears at Maslins Beach

Robin Binney thinking he's got the 'Big One'

'Gang Wars', our house from our 'Fort' in the pine tree

Photographing the wedgetailed eagle nest at Yundi

Myself and Trevor Nottage camping at 'Glen Shera'

Myself, Paul Chenoweth and Allan Oakley camping at Yundi

'Shooting my first kangaroo – A bitter sweet experience'

Chapter 12

Concerts

I was always looking for different ways to make money. Some of my earliest remuneration came from selling Pomegranates, as we had a big tree below the house with its roots in our kitchen drain. I sold them for a penny each, but could see I would never be a millionaire out of them.

Then I had the idea of Saturday morning concerts, and offered Trevor Nottage a share in the business.

The first couple of Saturdays we worked ourselves to the bone (including Dianne who I conscripted as unpaid labour, as she would always do everything I asked of her!)

We did handstands, Trevor read his self-written stories on 'Sin land', and I read from my self-constructed comics about a little bloke called 'Squibby', and various other stuff, but we could see we were losing the crowd's attention. They had to pay a couple of pence to attend.

I thought of a radical idea and put it to Trevor, who agreed. At the finish of the second concert I told the 'crowd' that next week there would be a special act that I had been working on, and not to miss it – tell your friends. They must have, because the next Saturday morning the front lawn was nearly full, with everyone looking expectant.

Our 'stage' was the front verandah. The house was built on a slope, so the top side of the verandah was on the ground, and the bottom end was over a metre in height. It was made of jarrah boards with cracks between them. Trevor was noticeably absent. I made the announcement that I had become a crack shot with the air gun and that I was about to perform a feat that would amaze them.

On the end of the verandah Dianne had set up a 'target', which was a matchbox sitting on an empty paint tin.

The crowd couldn't see it, but attached to the back of the matchbox was a piece of cotton, going down through a crack in the verandah. Under the verandah was Trevor, who had the cotton in his hand.

I walked up to the other end of the verandah where my air gun leant against the wall. By it was one of Mum's old bedroom mirrors, with a handle on it. I picked both up, and with due ceremony faced the crowd, dramatically stating that the special act was about to start.

I asked for total silence, and got it. I then stood with my back to the target, making out to load the air gun. Picking up the mirror in my left hand, I held it up so that the matchbox came into view. I then placed the air gun over my right shoulder and took careful aim at the matchbox, before squeezing the trigger.

The air gun makes the same noise loaded or empty, and as the report sounded, the matchbox flew off the end of the verandah. There was thunderous applause (relatively) and I felt very, very important. Didn't seem to bother my conscience. Before the show finished, I told everyone to tell more people as there would be even more skillful shooting next week.

I couldn't wait for the week to pass. Trevor wanted a go on the air gun, but I explained to him that you could only have one famous marksman at any one time. He wasn't happy, but giving him half the takings seemed to improve his demeanor.

Next Saturday morning the lawn couldn't hold everyone, and there were kids standing, leaning on the brush fence from out on the footpath. I noticed there were some older boys as well, including John Ellis and Stan Smith, and realized my fame was spreading (or, they 'smelt a rat'!)

Like last week, Trevor was out of sight under the verandah. I performed the same act as before and it went off well. Dianne reset the matchbox, and nobody could see that there was no hole in it where the slug should have hit. I then informed the crowd dramatically that I would attempt a trick shot that never before had been attempted. A hush descended over the crowd, the only noise being Colin Ledgard, our neighbor across the road, having a coughing fit.

Taking the air gun in my right hand, I spread my legs, bent over and poked the gun between my legs, taking a wobbly aim on the target. Suddenly the matchbox was jerked off the paint tin, disappearing off the end of the verandah – before I'd fired the gun!

There was an uproar, with the older boys over the fence yelling out that I was a cheat.

Next thing there was someone's mother telling me that I must return all the money, and then Mum appeared, and said that was what had to be done. I was pretty embarrassed, and furious with Trevor. He had disappeared, and I never was sure if he had 'set me up' out of spite, or if it was a mistake. There was a bit said for a week or so, but kids' memories are short and things soon returned to normal. That was the end of my 'show business' career however.

***

Chapter 13

Royce

Most communities have at least one member who is' mentally retarded'. In the cities, it could probably be said that these unfortunate people have a harder life than their counterparts in country towns. In McLaren Vale there was such a person called Royce (pronounced Roysey) Wickham. He was a great character, and I am sure pretty well all of the towns' people appreciated him – and went out of their way to be kind to him. Like my whippet, Jock, he had a 'town round'. He was a man of around fifty, shortish with a thatch of thin sandy hair. Usually wore a grey work shirt (summer and winter) and old grey work pants with braces.

At least one night of the week, usually when we were having tea, he would appear at our back door and give his distinctive call. Dad would go to the back door and Royce would often respond with 'kick a in a arse', giving his funny grin at the same time.

He was a regular up at the Four Square Store where he would spend hours out the back stacking empty drink bottles in crates. Other times he would pick up cans and other litter around the streets, putting them in an old bag he carried over his shoulder.

One day I did a stupid inexcusable thing that really upset me. He was walking down the footpath past our house. For no particular reason, I picked up a green pinecone, and threw it at Royce. It struck him on the top of his head, drawing blood. He put his hand on his head and I could tell it had really hurt him. I hid behind the fence so that he couldn't see me. I didn't tell anyone about it, and my conscience gave me a hard time for some time afterwards.

Probably the thing that Royce would be most remembered for was this. On Saturday afternoons there were trots held at Victor Harbour, and late in the afternoon all the traffic would be heading through McLaren Vale, back to Adelaide. Just before the traffic reached McLaren Vale, Royce would walk up to Bosworths Garage, where the Kangarilla Road joined the Main South Road. He took with him a yard broom, and would walk down the white line in the middle of the road – sweeping it!

The first cars would arrive, frantically tooting their horns, but Royce completely ignored them. Quite often there would be a line of fifty or sixty cars, stretching back out of sight, some sounding their horns, others mystified as to what the hold-up was. Sometimes a driver would get out to speak to Royce, who would raise his broom above his head, walk toward the startled driver, yelling "kick a in a arse".

People had no idea how to deal with him.
In due course the local policeman (Hartley Paine) would come up and ask Royce if he would get off the road. Royce always obeyed with his funny little smile, and the traffic would flow freely once again. This went on for years.

***

Chapter 14

Boarding School

When I was thirteen, Dad told me one evening that I was to be sent to Prince Alfred College as a boarder – or to be more precise, as a weekly boarder, which meant I could come home on weekends. I was devastated. The thought of being sent away from home upset me no end. I had my mates at McLaren Vale and was enjoying life, and had no desire to change things. Dad's father (Grandpa Ellis) and Dad both went to this school, and I suppose Dad was keen to keep the tradition going, but I didn't want a bar of it. In the end though, I realized that Dad had his mind set on it, and reluctantly accepted my fate.

There was a visit to the school prior to the start of term, and the family was shown around. It was all weird to me, and didn't improve my enthusiasm one little bit. There were other boys being shown around as well, and I did notice that not many of them showed any signs of excitement, which was some small consolation.

Finally the day came when Dad and Mum drove me into Adelaide, and dropped me off at the school. It was a Sunday afternoon. They left me at the main entrance to the boarding house, with several other boys. The Housemaster took us in tow, leading us up steps to the third storey where our dormitories were. On this floor were three dormitories with twelve beds in each, with the shower/ toilets along one end. At the head of the dormitories were a number of prefects 'studies'. These prefects were directly in charge of us, like our jailers, and had extraordinary powers of discipline.

I stowed my clothes in a cupboard, and like the other boys, wandered around like lost sheep. I was pleased that they all seemed to be country lads, but I was feeling homesick and out of my element.

After a while a bell rang, and someone told us to go down to the dining room for the evening meal. This was a large room with an adjoining kitchen on the ground floor. Large, because it had to accommodate one hundred and twenty five boarders and a number of live-in masters (teachers). That night we had a cold serve with a desert of fruit and custard. Soon after, we were herded back up to our dormitories and in bed by eight thirty.

We were rudely awoken by a bell at six thirty and dragged ourselves out of bed. There were a few that were still asleep, and a prefect (a boy of sixteen or seventeen) came along and unceremoniously stripped back the bedclothes, hollering at the luckless kid to get out of bed. I was glad I was already up. Down to breakfast of porridge and eggs and bacon, with very little talking while we were eating. Not because it was banned, but more because we hardly knew each other.

We were then drafted off to our classrooms. I can't remember how it was worked out, but I was sent to Form C, which was definitely where you wouldn't find the academics. The 'bright lights' were in Form A. Our class teacher introduced himself, and as we undertook different lessons we met an assortment of different Masters, as they were called. They all wore black gowns that immediately reminded me of Batman and Robin comics. The gowns made them look very formidable.

There was a bell for recess time, and we were all allowed to go to the tuck shop and purchase something. I soon became a cream bun addict. More lessons, an hour for lunch, then finally school out at quarter to four, and what a relief that was. Short-lived though, because after the evening meal we were sent back to our classrooms for what was called Night school. Just homework, but there is nothing more depressing to me than being in a classroom in the evening. A Housemaster supervised us while we attended (struggled) with our homework.

This was the weekly routine, until Friday afternoon. When the bell rang, I flew out of the classroom, up to my dormitory, grabbed my bag, and headed for the railway station. Much to the envy of other boys. Out of the one hundred and twenty five boarders, there was less than half a dozen of us that were weekly boarders. McLaren Vale was only twenty five miles from Adelaide, making this possible.

I can't describe the relief and excitement I felt when I boarded the Willunga train, and started steaming south through the suburbs. Then into the country. I loved going through the little (then) country towns of Reynella, Morphett Vale, Hackham, Noarlunga, and finally to my very familiar stomping ground of the McLaren Vale railway station. I was delighted to see my little sister Dianne, faithfully waiting for me on the station platform, and together we walked up through our paddock to the house, with big hugs from Mum and Dad.

I don't remember that particular weekend too clearly, but I would have spent some of it detailing my experiences to some of my mates.

But the downside of this was, as the Sunday afternoon wore on, I had to prepare myself to get back on the train, heading back to 'jail' as I called it. I felt pretty low that first Sunday, returning to the school. However, as the school term progressed I started to make some mates at the school, and going back wasn't quite such a lonely experience.

We all gradually became immersed into new activities, like the school cadets, and trying out for different sports. However, because I used to disappear at weekends, I didn't play sport for the school. I used to play, at various times, tennis, cricket and football for McLaren Vale. Average at all of them, but not starring in any.

Then, around halfway through the first term, I became the willing victim of a huge practical joke. Thinking back, it was probably this experience that got me going in my own 'career' as a practical joker.

On the back verandah of the boarding house there was a general notice board that we were all required to read regularly. One day I went to do this, and the thing that jumped out at me from the board was a notice "Marble Players Wanted". I was a very handy marble player, and still had my collection of 'cats eyes' and other types of marbles. The notice said that the school wanted to form an "Intercollegiate Marble Team", and that anyone interested should assemble on the back oval at four thirty the following afternoon.

I was immediately interested, because I was good at this. I was one of the first to arrive, and soon there was a group of around twenty boys. Then one of the prefects arrived, and explained that he was going to conduct a series of trials in order to pick a team of four, and a team captain. He had with him a bag of marbles, and gave us all half a dozen each. We were then put through our trials, and although I was far from perfect, I couldn't help but notice that I seemed to be the best of the bunch. I couldn't believe it, and redoubled my enthusiasm. After several sessions, four boys were picked out, and to my joy I was announced as Captain. For the first time since I arrived at this school, I was noticed. As I walked around, different boys (older boys who would never even notice us first years) would say "Good on you Ellis" or similar comments. I had never felt so important in all my life. That weekend I couldn't wait to get home to tell my mates and family. I failed to see the twinkle in Dad's eye as he congratulated me. For a few short weeks I rode the crest of this wave, with regular marble practice on the back oval. We always had an audience, and if there were any derogative comments, they would have gone over my head anyway. The prefect 'coach' in charge told us that anytime we required extra marbles (they would sometimes break or get lost or pinched) we could go to the Bursar and purchase them for tuppence halfpenny each.

One fatal afternoon I needed to buy a couple of extras, and went along to the Bursar's office. I knocked on the door, and a voice said "come" and in I went. The very severe looking Bursar was sitting behind his desk, writing something. He looked up, asking what I wanted. "Sir" I said, "Could I please have fivepence worth of marbles?" He stared at me for a second or two, then practically collapsed in mirth. He laughed 'til tears ran down his cheeks. Finally he stopped and said "Get out boy, you've been had", before resuming his laughter. I slunk out of this office, closed the door behind me, and just stood there as the terrible realisation sunk in. I had been 'had' alright, in capital letters. I went up to my dormitory, lay on my bed, filled with desolation. That night I went through the motion of eating and night school like a zombie, and next day was one of the worst I could remember.

The word soon got out, and before the day's end, my nickname was 'Fivepence'. I simply had to wear it. A few of my mates were sympathetic, but I was suddenly one of the best known kids in the whole school for all the wrong reasons. I went home that weekend with my tail between my legs. When I told Dad he commiserated with me, but never let on until much later, that he knew all along.

Anyway, I had no option but to weather the storm, and gradually my embarrassment subsided, to be replaced with a steely determination to be on the 'dealing out' end of the practical joke department.

I found the school cadets an interesting experience, having always had an interest in things to do with guns and military. Spent most of my time polishing brass and cleaning my boots. That never seemed good enough for the 'officers', who were mostly prefects in uniform.

An interesting thing happened one day during hand grenade practice. The distance you could throw a hand grenade was a big factor and all of us tried to outdo one another. The 'officer' kept having a go at me to throw it further, and was standing out to the side of where I was throwing it. Making a huge effort to throw it the maximum distance, it spun sideways out of my hand, flying across and cracked the officer on the shin. His hat flew off and he hopped around on one leg cursing me in no uncertain terms.

Pity it wasn't 'live', I thought, and for that little effort I had to stand to attention out in the sun for an hour. It's a bit of a 'toss up' who the enemy is in those situations.

Because I was a fanatical 'Birdo', I started up a group called grandly the Australian Forresters Union. I managed to coerce half a dozen blokes into supposedly starting a branch in each of their home towns. It all looked good on paper, showing we had branches in Keith, Bordertown, Strathalbyn, Peake, Beaulah in Victoria and Elkedra Station in the Northern Territory. All these blokes appeared very earnest about conscripting local members, and I could see myself giving up school and running the AFU full time!

In reality nothing really happened, which was a pity, because I had all sorts of certification designed, and written up by hand, including a 'magazine' called the 'Cassowary'. Eventually the whole show folded.

Not so my interest in ornithology. I was a regular visitor after school to the ornithology department of the South Australian Museum. The resident Curator of Birds, Herb Condon, became a good friend, and encouraged me a lot.

One school holidays, I accompanied a mate, Ron Goudie, over to his home at Beaulah, in the north west of Victoria. His father owned a stock and station agency. It was a very memorable three weeks. The Yarryambiak Creek was flooding, and we spent a lot of time along its banks, birding, yabbying and generally messing around. The last week we went up to the River Murray near Mildura which was experiencing its biggest flood in the century. An old fisherman (Bob), a mate of Ron and Phil's father, had moved his camp back to the edge of the floodwaters. We had a great week camped there, in boats and on foot. It was while here that I had a lot to do with a flock of white-winged choughs, and wrote an article about their feeding habits, that was published in the EMU. This was the official magazine of the

Royal Australasian Ornithological Society, and I was tickled pink about this. Choughs build a large mud nest, and have a number of regular feeding spots in their territory, which they visit each day. One of these happened to be Bob's fowlyard, where I was able to observe them at close quarters. This visit was my first real association with the Murray River, and was the catalyst for a lifelong love affair with the mighty river.

Another hugely exciting time was a holiday spent with a couple of Northern Territory mates (Dennis and Roy Driver) on their cattle station Elkedra. This began with a journey on 'the Ghan' train to Alice Springs. We boarded the train in Adelaide, and after changing at Port Pirie settled down in our sleeper compartments. I awoke next morning and looked out the window at the siding of Parachilna on the western side of the Flinders Ranges. This was my first introduction to the outback of Australia, and I was immediately 'hooked'.

We had a lot of fun on that train. There were a lot of boarding school kids returning to stations and Alice Springs.

Girls were a big preoccupation for us blokes, and much of our time and energy was taken up in this area. Dennis in particular was 'chasing' Janne Hargraves, who he eventually married and is still married to.

I remember a very amusing incident when the Ghan pulled into the little town of Finke near the NT – SA border. The publican obviously had a very good racket going with the engine crew on the train. It was only a short stop there. Most of the passengers rushed over to the pub to buy beer. The 'long necks' (large bottles) were done up in flimsy brown paper bags, with half a dozen in each. Just before the appointed time of departure, the train sounded its whistle, and began moving slowly forward. Everyone panicked and began rushing out of the pub, with many of the bags splitting, spilling out the bottles. Many were so scared of missing the train, which kept sounding its whistle, that they didn't try to pick up their lost bottles. As they raced to the train, the publican and a mate came out of the pub, picked up the bottles on the ground and returned to the pub.

A very profitable hours action for him!

After some three days of fun and excitement, we reached the Alice, and I can still recall the wonderful atmosphere of the place. The boys' parents were there to meet us, and after spending a night in their town house, we drove the three hundred miles north east to Elkedra Station, a very remote place. The homestead was located on a large permanent waterhole of the Elkedra River. This was the beginning of three weeks of absolute adventure for me. I soon got to know the Station aborigines, a very happy group of people. The men worked in the stock camp, and some of the women in the homestead. One of the blokes, Nelson, was the mechanic. Their camp was down the creek a bit from the homestead. When the men wanted to go 'on walkabout' they would suddenly up and leave, often being away for weeks. This was tolerated and accepted as normal by the Drivers, even though it often caused the disruption of the muster. The aboriginals would get free clothing, tobacco and basic foodstuff from the Station Store, and John Driver funded the further education, and nursing career of some of the brighter of the kids. I am very glad that I experienced this situation, seeing the contrast between this and the present day turmoil of life in the settlements, which in many cases are not successful.

There was one memorable day when I accompanied a man called Charlie on a hunting expedition. He had several dogs and a couple of killing boomerangs. After an hour or so he spotted a Euro in the shade of a Eucalypt near some low rocky hills. Motioning me to remain, he approached the euro, stopping whenever the animal looked up from feeding. His dogs kept behind him.

When he was within about forty metres of the euro, he threw one of his boomerangs, which struck the euro on the upper neck. It appeared stunned, and Charlie set the dogs on to it, before going in and dispatching it with a blow to the head. After gutting it, he hoisted it on top of his head, carrying this heavy load back to the camp several kilometres away, with only a couple of spells in between. Very impressive.

I spent a week in the stock camp, was given a horse called Gypsy, and thoroughly enjoyed this experience.

At the homestead each morning and evening, Spinifex pigeons would emerge from the low rocky spinifex clad hills, making their way to the waterhole. I spent quite a bit of time observing them, and wrote an article on them, which was also published in the 'Emu'. Finally the holiday came to an end, and we flew back to school from Adelaide. Interesting, but not as exciting as the train.

Back to 'jail' as we used to say, with all the frustrations of school work. I found that to make life more bearable, I had to indulge in a bit of 'mischief'.

I had a mate called Johnny Piper, who was nicknamed 'Thug'. He was a dark looking, thick set bloke, who was the champion 'shot putter'. He was coached by an elderly master called Mr Connell, who we used to call 'Toage'. It was supposedly a Japanese word that meant 'stink'. Toage used to stalk along in his black gown. He always shaved his head shorter than a crew cut, and wore rimless glasses – he had watery blue eyes, and used to preface all his utterances with 'uh uh uh' type sounds often accompanied by a clutching of his chin. A very unusual man and one wide open to being 'got at'.

He used to take us for history once a week. I don't think his heart was in it, because most times he would set us some reading or essays, and then sit at his desk and read himself. He was also fairly deaf.

One day we all started to make a low humming noise, gradually increasing the volume until it reached Toage's hearing. He looked up, listening, then asked "What's that noise?" One of us said "I think it's a steam roller doing road works out in Little Copper Street, sir". He seemed satisfied, and after continuing for a while, we let the humming die off.

One of his real phobias was kids' kitbags that were left in the aisles. He would flick his beady eyes at them, then savouring the moment, move into position so that he could 'address' the bag. He would then give a little hop, skip and jump, before giving the bag an almighty boot, sending it sliding down the aisle and into the back wall. Then he would clutch his chin, saying "Uh uh, you can keep that out of the aisle, and under your desk!" We used to get sick of opening up our bags after these assaults, and often finding severe damage like caved in vegemite sandwiches, etc. in our lunches. So mostly we kept our bags under our desks. We reckoned Toage really regretted not being able to kick a bag, because he would enter the classroom his eyes would flick down the aisle hoping to see one.

So one day, Thug and I decided to give him one to kick. Being the champion shot put student, Thug had access to the heavy balls. He borrowed two of them, and taking everything out of my bag, put them in. I could hardly lift the bag off the floor it was so heavy. The next day I placed it in the aisle, near another lad's desk, and the whole class waited in breathless anticipation. Finally Toage entered the room and we noticed his eyes do their usual search of the bags. Then as his spied the lone bag, his face brightened and there was a spring in his step as he reached his desk.

Clutching his chin, he said "Uh uh, continue revision of Henry the Eighth". We lowered our heads, but kept Toage in sight. He could hardly contain himself, and eventually stood up from behind his desk. He walked toward the aisle, head bobbing like a bird in suppressed excitement. When he reached the aisle he looked at the kitbag for a second or two, then gave his little hop, skip and jump, before he sent his patent leather black shoe into the bag. Several things happened and didn't happen all at once.

Firstly the bag didn't move an inch, just sort of wobbled. Toage staggered, grabbing a desk for support, before letting out a terrible strangulated "Uhhhh Uhhhhh" type of noise. Then still emitting little grunts and whimpers, he limped back to his table.

Speaking for myself, the tears were running onto my page and I was struggling with suppressed mirth, but another feeling was coming to life in the back of my mind. It wasn't good, something to do with 'what goes around, comes around'. Anyway, next thing Toage gets himself together, and in a strained voice, said "Who was responsible?" Not a sound, not a murmur. "Uh, yes uh well, that's what I would expect – well you can all rot here as far as I'm concerned, until the culprits own up." Now everyone knows there is no honour amongst school boys, and here was a classic case. Most of the boys in the room turned and stared at Thug and I. That was enough for Toage. "Piper and Ellis" and looking particularly at Piper, his star shot put student, he went on "How very disappointing". Then, "Tonight, in my study at eight thirty". I went cold inside, the fun of the event completely erased. I knew what to expect.

That evening after night school, Thug and I had our shower, changed into our pyjamas (we knew this was mandatory) and went to Toage's study. (He was a resident Housemaster). Thug knocked on the door and a few seconds later, Toage opened it. "Good evening boys, a bit cool out tonight" or words of that nature. "Come on in". It was like we were being invited in for a cup of tea. We walked in and stood by his desk. I noticed on one wall there was a glass case with half a dozen canes displayed, like a gun rack. It wasn't really a cold night, but I shivered. He went on fiddling with some gear for several minutes before turning and fixing us with a watery stare. "Over the bed Piper, you will be first". Then Thug bent over the end of Toages bed so that his pyjama pants were tight on his backside. Toage went to his 'cane' cabinet, opened the door and stared for a number of seconds, considering. Finally he took out an evil piece of dowell about a metre long, and approached Thug. I stared in hopeless fascination. Toage then turned side on, gave a little jump, and swung the cane down hard onto Piper's bum. As I watched, a red stripe appeared. Toage wound up again, bought down the cane and a second stripe appeared. Thug didn't make a sound. He delivered three more cuts, which left five red stripes, the first two joining as the blood began to run. Toage stood up, saying "Now, get out", and Thug stood up, turned around and walked with a straight back out the door. I couldn't see his face.

"You next, Ellis, over the bed". In a sort of trance, I lay over the bed and closed my eyes. I heard a swishing sound, and felt a huge impact on my skinny little bum – but no real pain.

Then as the second stroke struck, I felt the first one – absolute agony. I only received three, because he correctly guessed that I was the 'offsider' in this particular operation. As I walked out the door, the tears were streaming down my face and my whole rear end was consumed in agony. I returned to the darkened dormitory, and crawled under the covers. It was a high price to pay. But life goes on.

Some time later, Thug and I had our attention drawn to a boy in the top A Form, who was a terrible snob. He was the son of one of the state's great academics, and following in his footsteps. Nothing wrong with that, but we felt it was up to us to try and improve his demeanor – very arrogant, among other things. So we studied his behaviour for a while, looking for his 'Achilles heel'. We noted that on Thursdays, his class' last lesson was Chemistry, where everyone vacated the room and went to the chemistry laboratory.

This boy, Michael, would leave his kitbag, full up with homework books, by the side of his desk. When the chemistry lesson finished, he would rush back into the classroom, pick up his bag on the run, and head off to catch a bus, with only minutes to spare.

Here was the situation we were looking for. One night after school, on my way back from the museum, I purchased some galvanized clouts (a flat headed nail). Waiting until the Thursday, and having borrowed a hammer from the carpentry workshop, Thug excused himself from our class, saying he had to go to the toilet. Instead he went to Form A's empty classroom. He took all of the books out of Michael's bag, nailed it to the floor with about twenty clouts, replaced the books and did up the bag. He came back to class and five minutes before the bell, I obtained permission to leave the room. I went to Form A and standing nearby so that I could observe the scene, I waited. The final bell went and a stampede of boys descended on the classroom, Michael at the forefront. He didn't disappoint. Hardly breaking his stride, he grabbed the handle of his bag. His pace was only momentarily checked as the bag (or the top side, back and front) let go with a ripping noise. Michael stumbled, and held up his bottomless bag in disbelief. He gawked at the spilt books on the floor. The he stooped down, gathered most of them up in his arms, and ran awkwardly to catch the bus. I slid down the wall, laughing fit to kill. One or two had seen the debacle, but it had gone largely unnoticed. Thug soon arrived and when I described the scene, we both descended to the floor.

Now, some may think that the incident would improve the way Michael conducted himself. Others would think, well why should it? And they were right, no change whatsoever. What happened was that Michael soon had a brand new kitbag, and Thug reported that the following week Michael actually stopped at his desk (after chemistry), lifted his bag up to check it was intact, then took off for his bus.

We let it go for a couple of weeks. Then I excused myself in the last lesson, going to Michael's classroom. I grabbed a two gallon container of water where I had planted it, on the way. Going to Michael's bag, I emptied the books into an old calico bag, and hid them up the back of the classroom. I poured the water into the brand new bag, which are actually watertight. I filled it up and closed it, before leaving for my classroom. Thug got reluctant permission to leave just before the bell, and went to observe. The bell rang and Michael rushed into the room, picked up the bag as was his fashion, and then took off. This time, Thug followed him. Michael got on the bus and sat next to a little old lady in a black dress. Thug got on, standing at the back of the bus.

Immediately, with study on his mind, Michael opened the bag on his lap. A geyser of water shot up, drenching both Michael and the little old lady. She was furious and abused him in no uncertain manner. Thug got off at the next spot, still splitting his sides.

The bottom line to this story is that the only thing that changed with Michael was that after these incidents, he would open his bag, take the books out, check the bag, put them in again, and then run a lot faster to make his bus on time. We had at least tried.

The weekends were very precious, and of course, the school holidays best of all. At various times, I had different mates out to stay, like the Driver brothers, Ron Goudie and Des Masters. Mum would sometimes do their washing for them, and she was amazed at one time to find that Roy Driver had been wearing a pair of socks for six weeks! For some reason I can't remember. Anyway, we would quite often go camping, mostly with mates of mine from McLaren Vale.

The Onkaparinga River featured a lot in my childhood. It was only a few miles to the north of McLaren Vale, and between Clarendon and Noarlunga ran through a very rugged gorge. We would do day walks up there, overnight camps, or on occasion spend three or four days camped up there. I still have large heavy exercise books where I recorded birds that we saw, and diaries of our camps. Sometimes Dad would drop us up near the gorge by car to save us lugging all our gear up, and a couple of times he dropped us at Clarendon to walk down the gorge, picking us up at Noarlunga a few days later. So we got to know the country pretty well.

From my records it is easy to see certain birds that were in the area then, are no longer there now. Birds like the Brown Tree Creeper and Diamond Firetail are two that come to mind.

On one occasion we carried up four 4 gallon drums and built a raft, our idea being to follow the river from Long Hole down to Noarlunga, a distance of about three miles. The river was in flood at the time. We built the raft alright, and just taking our lunch with us, set off in the floodwaters. It was pretty scary with three of us on board, and very unstable. We only got to the end of Long Hole (a large waterhole) where it ran into 'channel', and got jammed under a tree that had fallen across the river. We lost all our lunches, and were probably lucky that no one lost their life as well. That was the end of the raft idea.

There was an incident in the boarding house that would have done the school a fair bit of damage if it had got into the papers. One Sunday night I arrived back at the school, and as usual headed up to my dormitory to go to bed. Bit of a yarn to the blokes, and duly went to sleep. About midnight I woke up to find the lights on and blearily looking around I noticed that half the boys weren't in their beds. Peter Skipworth (Ponderous), who was in the bed next to me, was sitting up. He was as mystified as me. Most of the activity seemed to be focused out on the landing where the bathrooms and toilets were, so we got out of bed and went out for a look. The sight that met my eyes was one that I'll never forget – or the smell!

It seemed like most of the boarding house had the shits. Every available bit of space was taken up. The four toilets had occupants and all of the baths had kids sitting on the edges filling up the baths, as did each of the wash basins. I couldn't believe it. Next thing, 'Ponderous' flew past me, on a desperate mission, as he became afflicted. I expected trouble myself, but felt good as gold. As I moved along the landing, I observed an example of where politeness doesn't pay off. A little bloke must have been waiting in a queue at one of the toilets. Finally it was his turn. He rushed into the toilet and as he dropped his strides and swung around, he did it all around the wall! It was disgusting, but sort of surreal.

I got caught up in the surge of boys heading down the stairs to escape the stench. However, as usual, the door to the next floor was locked. Dozens of kids began banging on the door and yelling out. Now, through the door lived a very unpopular housemaster, with the nickname of 'Pampas' (he had a bald head, and a large black Mexican type moustache).

He must have thought there was a riot, and opened the door with a cane in his hand. He was literally 'flattened' as dozens of boys scrambled over him.

We headed on down the stairs, and poured out on to the front oval, and fresh air. In due course, order was restored by prefects and housemasters, but we spent the rest of the night sleeping on the floor in the library and other places.

There was a good reason why myself and the few other weekly boarders were not affected. Apparently the mayonnaise on the Sunday night cold serve was 'off', and weekly boarders returned after the evening meal. Several of the kitchen maids were sacked, we heard, and felt a bit sorry for them. It was a night to remember.

A few months before I left the school in 1957, I took some interesting photographs. I had been a keen photographer since I was about ten, starting off with the old Brownie Box Camera. Then there was a great leap in technology. Dad bought me a camera for Christmas, called an 'Agfa Clack' – one of the first eye level viewfinder cameras. I absolutely loved that camera, and carried it in my kitbag.

Because I was no academic genius, I sat right up in the back row of my class. One day our class teacher (Desert Head) was busy 'adjusting' (caning) a few of the boys. He had this specially designed piece of apparatus made out of car tyre, and shaped like a table tennis bat.

He used this in preference to a cane, maybe because it fitted easily into his briefcase. Anyway, as he administered his punishment to various boys, I took the Agfa Clack out of my bag, and took a series of 'action shots'. I reasoned that I could probably do a tap dance on top of my desk while he was 'adjusting' these boys, and he wouldn't have noticed.

A few days later, I took some of another master as well. [These photographs caused a lot of interest when I attended a school reunion about ten years ago – I enlarged four photographs with a caption underneath, stating 'Paying clients being adjusted by the establishment'. About halfway through the black tie dinner, a bell sounded, and I was asked to join the hierarchy at the head table. After all those years, the first thing that went through my head was "Shit, I'm going to get the cane!" They were just a bit intrigued as to how I got away with taking these photographs.]

The day I left the school I showed 'Desert Head' the pictures. His face went bright pink, and his eyes nearly popped out. It was a bit of satisfaction as I walked out the gate. Having said all that, it was (is) a very good school, with a lot of dedicated teachers, and it didn't do me any harm.

Unless you were a real 'Goody Goody Two Shoes', prefects were a constant hazard. In many cases, they were an example of too much power, too early. The fact that they could administer corporal punishment was like a licence to kill. They were not allowed to own or use canes, their recommended dispenser of justice being a leather slipper. Curiously, when the giant tech toothbrush came on to the market, these were also added to their arsenal, although I doubt they would have been recommended by the hierarchy. You might think it would be hard to inflict pain with a toothbrush, well you'd be wrong. They would get you to bend over the bed in the usual fashion, then honing into a spot (checkered pyjama pants were probable of great use to them) on your rear end, they would bend the giant tech back as far as it would bend, and let it go. Half a dozen of them on the same small area was agony, I can tell you. It was mainly the more sadistic prefects that used this 'weapon'. However, there were other ways to inflict punishment on us hapless youths apart from belting our bums.

There was one very large, heavy prefect that used to go by the name of Bull Frog (his younger brother was called 'Tadpole'). Like the rest of them, he had to do night school, but theirs finished after we were in bed and asleep. Wrapping a towel around his large loins, he would come thundering through our dormitory on his way to a shower, making as much noise as possible.

We put up with this for a while, but then the germ of an idea formed in my little brain. Without telling anyone, each night I pushed my bed out an inch or two. It took five nights before the large castor on the end of my bed coincided with his flight path.

As he flew into the air, he screamed like a stuck pig, before he crashed on to the floor several beds past me. Even while he was still airborne, I hopped out in the dark and pulled my bed in.

When Bull Frog staggered to his fee, whimpering like a baby and switched on the light, twelve innocent lads appeared like they were dead in bed, especially me. In a fury he ripped the blankets off a couple of beds, ranting and raving, but couldn't identify a victim. He hopped off vowing to get the culprit. I never told my mates it was me. He never ran through the dormitory again.

***

Chapter 15

First Jobs

When I left school, my main ambition was to be an ornithologist. However not only were there very few of these positions available at the time, my mathematical qualifications were totally inadequate. So I had a bit of an idea to become a stock and station agent. I arranged an interview with the 'Farmers Union', who agreed to employ me. However they said I was to spend six months, at least, at the head office in the city, before being sent to a country branch. I wasn't too keen, but had no option, and eventually began my employment.

It was on the sixth floor of a building near Victoria Square, in the middle of Adelaide. I was given a little desk (like a school desk) next to a big fat bloke with a bald head sitting at his big desk. All day long he would pass these huge ledgers down to me that I had to go through, writing down simple mundane stuff regarding Farmers Union clients. It was dead boring and didn't change from day to day. As well as that he used to drop these terrible farts. Such things are supposed to rise but these didn't and I copped them. 'Smoko' consisted of a cup of tea and sweet biscuit, but I had to keep working. Lunch was the only good part of the day, and I used to buy it at a nearby cafe, then go out into Victoria Square and eat it. (In the relatively fresh air!)

I didn't have any mates to break the boredom, the only pleasure being checking out the sheilas, of which there was a never ending supply. Not that it did me any good.

One other bit of a bright spot was at certain times the big fat bloke would disappear somewhere for an hour at a time. Across the lane was another building with a lot of young female typists. Myself and another young bloke used to shoot paper clips across at the other building with large rubber bands. A bit pathetic really, but that's what I had to do to keep my sanity.

After six weeks I talked Dad into agreeing to me quitting. I then got a job as a storeman at the merchandise department of the McLaren Vale Fruitpackers. At the same time I was making enquiries about going jackerooing and also doing a wool classers course. The sixteen months or so that I spent at the 'packers' was a very enjoyable part of my early years.

I was sixteen years old. There were five of us in the large store. The boss was Angas MacLachlan, with senior members being Eddie Kemp, Victor Wright and David Rehn, one of my mates, Robin Binney had been working there for a year, and myself on the bottom rung of the ladder. We had a good boss, and really every day was a day to be looked forward to. The work was interesting enough, but it was interspersed with 'Fun'. Also in the complex were two office girls, Judith Culley and Wendy Poole, the accountant Jack Scales, the big boss Roy Hall and in the motor garage, Fred Osmond and Merv Crowhurst, with Duff Sigston the apprentice. Plus a couple of permanent blokes in the packing shed.

Motorbikes

I had my drivers licence, and was keen to get a car, but Dad reckoned I had to wait a year, or get a motorbike. So I saved my money and bought a little BSA Bantam. At the same time a lot of my mates had motorbikes (mostly Bantams), and most weekends we would be riding them around the back tracks, or down to the beach. There was an established dirt track circuit out at McLaren Flat, and we spent a fair bit of time there as well. From Bantams, I graduated to a Jawa, which was broken down most of the time, but then I got hold of a very exciting little bike – a 197cc Ambassador. A short stubby bike, with girder forks. This was a real power plant, and I'm lucky to be here writing this. I really loved that bike. Then it was into four strokes, and for a short time I had a 250cc BSA. When Robin Binney arrived at work one day in a sleek looking 600cc Featherbed Norton, I decided on a 'big bike' and a few weeks later bought a 500cc VG Ariel. I had this bike until I went bush in 1960.

I used to ride my BSA Bantam to work, and leave it propped up against the front of the building. The first afternoon, I went out to ride home, but it wouldn't start. So I tried to 'run start' it, by pushing it along the road, in gear, with the clutch lever held in. When I had a bit of speed I would jump sideways on to the seat, simultaneously letting out the clutch lever. Still wouldn't go. I ended up right down by Joe Chapman' s, practically worn out, when along came Fred Osmond, from the Packers Garage. Fred mucked around for a couple of seconds, putting himself between me and what he was doing to the bike. Then he got on, gave it one kick and it started, good as gold.

Next afternoon the same thing happened, and by the time I reached the bottom end of the town I was ready to burn the bike. Then, Fred came along and performed the same rituals as the day before. It started.

On the third afternoon it wouldn't start again. I was just about to tear my hair out, when a voice from the open office window called out "Try checking the spark plug Rexy boy". I did, and the lead was off. The rotten buggers had been taking it off each night, just before I knocked off, and I hadn't been smart enough to 'twig'. Who needs mates like that!

My other mania was Firearms. Starting off with .22 rifles of various types, I would sell them and buy heavier calibres, the first one being a .303 Jungle carbine. I would have several at once including shotguns.

In between my bird watching, I would do a fair bit of shooting, mostly foxes, rabbits and hares (although I had a soft spot for them).

A few of us went away a couple of times shooting kangaroos. I then got a liking for lever action rifles, and had at different times a 32.20 and a Martini action 310. Each time I bought a firearm I would go and register it at the local police station. On one occasion when I walked in the door, the policeman (Hartley Paine) said to me that if I bought any more that year, I would have to obtain a secondhand dealers licence, so I took it easy for a while.

We used to do a bit of fishing, although I wasn't all that keen on it. One day a few of us went over to Yorke Peninsula in Robin Binney' s little Morris Minor (he had sold his Norton). Robin was a very keen fisherman and had a couple of rods. I took my spear gun and flippers and goggles, and while Robin was fishing off the Wool Bay jetty, the rest of us were swimming under the jetty looking for fish. There was nothing around, but we could see Robin's hook and bait, as he periodically raised it and cast it out. I saw it land next to a jetty pilon and swam over, and very carefully attached the hook to a cross piece of timber, taking the weight off the line as I did so. When it was attached, I gave the line a big jag. Next thing Robin was trying to land the biggest fish he had ever hooked! It was a classic.

Back at work, our favourite part of every day was morning 'smoko'. We would all cluster around Eddy Kemp' s desk, because there was a large window in front of it that looked out across the street toward the pub. Judith or Wendy used to deliver our cups of tea and biscuits to us.

Ern Oakley

There was a great character out at McLaren Flat called Ern Oakley, (there was a lot of characters in the McLaren Flat area - including some people who had never even been to Adelaide!) and once a week he used to come into 'the Vale', lying across the back of his two-wheeled cart (horse drawn). On this occasion the horse and cart passed our window, with the reins dragging, but no Ern! Five minutes later he slouched past covered in dust and minus a bit of skin. He had gone to sleep and fallen off!

His weekly trips into the Vale were mostly to deliver freshly trapped rabbits to the pub. One day apparently the publican (Ernie Bruce) had had a go at him about the rabbits not being fresh enough, and Ern stalked out in a rage. The next afternoon, just before six o'clock closing, he pushed his way through the crowd towards the bar with the bag and started vigorously shaking it. As half a dozen live rabbits ran out along the bar, Ern yelled at Ernie Bruce" Are these fresh enough for you then?" Turning around he headed off back to McLaren Flat, to the huge enjoyment of the bar.

Ern would often have too much to drink. At closing time, he would get himself out to his cart and patiently waiting horse, pull himself on to the back and instantly pass out. His horse would break into a steady walk, up through the Main Street, and all the way out to Ern's place at McLaren Flat. I never heard of Ern never getting home safely – he seemed to have more trouble when he was sober.

On another memorable occasion, there were a few in the pub, playing billiards, when a potted ball couldn't be retrieved. Ern went out to a box on his cart, opened the lid and withdrew a ferret. Taking it back into the bar, he sent it after the ball, inside the billiard table!

One hot summer he had just finished'borrowing' a couple of double iron gates from a large property in the foothills behind McLaren Flat. The owner came across him as he was heading off in his horse and cart. "You put those gates back Ern Oakley, or I'll get the police onto you". Ern pulled up, and looking at him replied, "It would be a lovely day for a fire, wouldn't it?" He continued on his way without any trouble.

Since our earliest days, myself as well as John Richard and Jim Ellis had access to a horse, an old mare called Smoke. Later on, I used to go up to a property in the hills owned by Brian Martin. He had horses, and would always loan me one to ride in the adjoining Kuitpo Forrest. I would take my lunch and spend most of the day riding around the fire breaks and logging tracks. On one occasion a big grey 'roo' jumped up under the horse's nose. He gave a snort and bolted, heading off the track into the Pines. I saw a horizontal branch coming up and half fell, half jumped out of the saddle. I landed heavily causing me to be winded, but otherwise was not seriously damaged. No sign of the horse, which headed home without me. By the time I made it back to Brian's, he was just about to leave to come and look for me.

A few of us became a bit interested in golf at one stage, but played a slightly different brand of it. It was called 'sniff and sip', and it worked like this. There was usually up to half a dozen of us including Robin Binney, Jim Ellis, Paul Chenowith and John Sears. We would carry a couple of bottles of either Rum or Port in the golf bags. Whoever won on a particular hole would have a'sip' of the beverage, while the losers would have a 'sniff'. What usually happened was that after a number of holes were played, the'sipper' would start to lose, and the situation would be reversed. Seemed like good fun at the time.

Girls began to be a big preoccupation with us blokes, and were on our minds a lot of the time. (All of the time!) At this period, a lot of us belonged to 'Rural Youth', and many weekends we would drive around the district wherever there were dances, or to Rural Youth Functions.

We were a bit of a casual sort of branch, and I know the Adelaide club didn't approve of a lot of our behaviour. On one occasion there was a big Rural Youth ball at the McLaren Vale hall. The Adelaide club were all there and their President was on the microphone holding forth to all in sundry – a lot of 'froth and bubble'. Snow Smith (ex the'Air Force Gang') who was a bit of a wild man, but a great character, had gate crashed the show. As the Adelaide President was waffling on, Snow sauntered down across the empty dance floor, and stood looking up at the self important Adelaide President. This unnerved the President, and he finished his diatribe prematurely. In the hush that followed, Snow drawled "Mate, I reckon that when you die, you'll come up as a noxious weed!" It brought the house down.

There was a family out the Flat called Attrills, and the kids consisted of George (a tough builder) and his four attractive sisters - Jean, Joan, Ann and Lois. All of these were members of Rural Youth, and we used to see a fair bit of each other. Anne used to work in the office at the Noarlunga Abattoirs, and each day would ride her bike around eight miles to and from her home to Noarlunga. One of my favourite times of the day at the Fruitpackers where I worked, was when Ann would ride past on her way home. She used to knock off a bit early. Being typical of most sixteen to seventeen year old boys, I hadn't yet plucked up courage to ask her out. It was only a few months before I went north jackerooing that I began taking her out, but that's another story.

The dances followed the usual format of all the blokes standing around the door with the girls sitting down around the sides of the hall. If we wanted a drink, we would have to go a certain distance, by law, from the hall. We would have our grog in a car, so there was a bit of coming and going between the hall and the cars. All of us blokes used to wear suits, with a lot of emphasis on ties, and getting your 'Windsor Knot' just right.

For most blokes, the object of the whole exercise was to try and yard up a sheila in order to 'take her home'. Some blokes would take the plunge and try and get that question sorted out early in the evening, but I think most of us used to try and rev our courage up through the course of the evening, and then desperately ask the question during the last dance. The only problem with that was if you got knocked back, you had very limited time for a second attempt.

There were those blokes that didn't dance, and only when the last dance was called, would they home in on some girl, get her on to the floor and hobble around like a kangaroo with a busted leg.

Australian men are often criticised or ridiculed for hanging around the entrance to halls, keeping separate from the women. Hard to know why, because they are not short of confidence in other areas. In reality they make it pretty hard for themselves. Consider this – when they want a dance, they have to focus on a certain female, then, like a heat seeking device, they make their way across the open desert of the dance floor, hoping desperately that someone doesn't beat them to the girl. If that's the case, they have two options. They either divert either side asking another girl (which isn't exactly a compliment to the girl) or swallow their pride and shuffle back to the door womanless. Yeah, it's not all beer and skittles.

One thing I'll relate here which will certainly shock and horrify the more genteel, but the truth is important, warts and all. Robert Hannan had an elder brother called Burnie, who was an absolute wizard with anything electrical. Robert approached me one day and took a device out of an old bag. It was simply a car generator with a handle on one end, with a piece of electrical wire coming out of the other end. Robert had this incredibly radical idea for this piece of apparatus at the next dance. It was showed to a select few, and we couldn't wait to try it out.

That Saturday night there was a big Rural Youth Ball in the McLaren Vale hall. About nine o'clock that night, a few of us went out the back of the hall to the gents toilet, an open air affair with a urinating trough consisting of an old piece of guttering. There were always gum leaves in the guttering, which made the job easier. We placed a piece of iron pipe in amongst these leaves (there was no lighting in the toilet which was also to our advantage) and attached the electrical wiring to it. The wiring ran back out of the trough, under the toilet wall and into the generator that we had in a hole in the hedge behind the toilet. From our position we couldn't see the 'victim', but we could certainly hear them coming and going!

What happened was this. When we heard a customer approaching the toilet one of us would start winding the handle on the generator. The bloke would approach the trough, get himself organised and start urinating. You don't need to be an apprentice electrician to understand what occurred next. Inside the hedge at 'mission control', we received a variety of 'feedback'. It ranged from "shit, shit, shit", with a noise like someone was trying to walk through the corrugated iron instead of the opening - to a simple "F......... Hell!"

George Attrill though, probably extended the damage wider than anyone else. I was in the hall at the time (we used to work shifts), when George, who had had a fair bit to drink, came rushing into the hall foyer with his fly open, shouting "Get a doctor, I've got the electricals". He was settled down, and next morning apparently though it was a bad dream. He didn't give up the grog though.

Meanwhile, back at the Fruitpackers, work was never dull. Being the youngest, I was often given a bit of a 'hard time' by the boys. Things like being sent out to the garage to ask Fred for a set of 'valve clearances' and stuff like that. But Robin Binney (who was often called 'Binge') did a terrible thing to me one day, probably being my most embarrassing moment so far.

I was serving a particularly 'precious' lady, who shall remain nameless. I hadn't long been there, and was still gaining my confidence, serving customers. While I was attending to this lady, in my peripheral vision I could see Binge crawling along the floor behind the counter, toward me. Couldn't imagine what he could be up to. He was well out of sight of the customer. When he was next to me he stopped, and I just tried to ignore him, and went on dealing with the customer. Next thing I was aware (as was the customer) of this foul smell. It was the mother of all farts - a silent sneaker of the worst kind! As far as the lady was concerned I was the perpetrator, and I went a deep beetroot red and was turned into a stuttering idiot. Fortunately, the transaction was coming to an end. I think the lady was going to pay cash but she just muttered "Charge it", and stalked out! That episode set my confidence back months.

I did a bit of grape picking that summer on the weekends. There was a large gang of us with Peter Rayner in charge.

Snow Smith was working with us, and providing most of the laughs.

One day Snow was kneeling down to get a low bunch when he spied a somewhat portly lady relieving herself a couple of rows away. As Snow walked back past us he muttered "I though the bloody cart had turned over!" Rough vineyard humour, but it passed the time.

On a few different occasions Dad would drop myself and a couple of mates out at Glen Shera, a six thousand acre sheep and cattle property in the Southern Mount Lofty Ranges, out the back of Myponga. There was still a lot of bush down there then, and it was a great place to camp. We always used to camp on a creek, engaging in the usual mix of bird watching, shooting and fishing. I shot my first kangaroo out there, very proud of myself then, but doesn't give me any pleasure to recall it now.

The heart rate was often going up as we avoided the numerous black snakes along the creek, but it kept us on our toes. One thing I do remember with great pleasure, were sightings of Pink Robins and Southern Emu Wrens. Sadly, both of these birds have gone from the region now.

One summer, we had a family holiday on Kangaroo Island, which was one of the best ever. We stayed at Elson's boarding house in Kingscote, and did trips out each day. At the time Dixon's Tours were running a day trip to Seal Bay, which is now a famous International destination. Seal Bay was a remote beach on the central South Coast of the island, accessed by a very rough sandy wheel truck.

In the morning an old Packard car pulled up in front of Elson's, and we met our driver/ guide, Rob, a bloke in his mid twenties. We drove down the gravel road to the Seal Bay turn off, and then headed along the sand truck. I think it took us a couple of hours, and I remember getting bogged several times. We finally arrived at Seal Bay, and looking down observed over a hundred sea lions on the beach, and in the water. We went down, and had a memorable experience. Rob took us into the water and we spent about an hour swimming with the sea lions. They actually seemed to enjoy us interacting with them, mainly females and younger animals. On occasion you could grab them by the tail, and they would take you for a wild ride, when you could manage to hang on long enough. It certainly gave us an appetite for lunch. This trip was significant in that I ended up living down the western end of Kangaroo Island for ten years, later in life. A special place.

***

Chapter 16

The Jubilee Train

It was the Jubilee Year, and we heard that a special Jubilee train was touring the state, and that it would be visiting McLaren Vale. We also heard that the train was booked out by the South Australian Railway Historical Society. We thought this was a bit rough so half a dozen of us decided to 'gate crash' the train. Our idea was to get on at the McLaren Vale Station, and try and ride it right into Adelaide. This is what happened.

We were waiting down at McLaren Vale Railway Station when the train pulled in from Willunga. It pulled up and many of the Railway Historical Society people got off, taking photographs, etc. A large crowd of local people hopped on board to view the many displays and exhibits – we were amongst them. When the train sounded its horn, the Railway Historical Society people came back on board, and the visitors (most of them) hopped off. As the train headed off we infiltrated the scene, trying to act like 'Railway buffs'. However after an hour or so, someone must have spotted us and dabbed us in to the guard.

We were up the front end of a crowded carriage, and saw a very red faced guard enter through the rear door, and looking straight at us. He began to make his way meaningfully through the crowd. We headed on into the next carriage. It was a very long train, and it took nearly ten minutes to walk through some of the carriages. We tried not to appear like 'fugitives', but it wasn't easy – the guard kept pursuing us, but at least he wasn't gaining.

We had a bit of a dilemma. One of the men involved in this little caper was Bob McBride, and he was following the train in his car, calling into the various stations in case we had to leave the train in a hurry.

In between Morphett Vale and Reynella, the line goes through a cutting with an uphill gradient, with a lot of olive trees growing near the track. At this stage we were in the front passenger carriage, and had a desperate idea to jump into the olive bushes as the train headed through the cutting. We were all gathered on the open platform at the front of the carriage. Even though the train had slowed down a fair bit, it would have taken a brave man to jump off.

Up ahead we could see the Reynella Railway Station coming up in a few minutes, but we could also see the guard was half way through the carriage, only minutes away from us. Looking ahead we could see Bob was there waiting for us. As the train slowed down we all bailed out and ran towards the car and hopped in. We could see the guard trying to write down Bob's number plate as we headed off, but we never heard anything more about it. We had had our Jubilee experience.

In 1960, I went jackerooing up at Lilydale Station in the north east of South Australia.

***

Books by **Rex Ellis**

$28.00

$19.99

$28.00

$29.99

$29.99

$28.00

$25.00

$29.99

$29.99 (novel)

$15.00

$24.99